LETTERS

ON

PRACTICAL SUBJECTS,

TO

A DAUGHTER.

BY WILLIAM B. SPRAGUE, D.D.

PASTOR OF THE SECOND PRESBYTERIAN CHURCH IN ALBANY.

ELEVENTH AMERICAN EDITION.

REVISED AND ENLARGED BY THE AUTHOR.

Harrisonburg, Virginia

SPRINKLE PUBLICATIONS

1987

Sprinkle Publications
P. O. Box 1094
Harrisonburg, Virginia 22801

CONTENTS.

PREFACE TO THE NEW EDITION

The reading of W. B. Sprague's, *Letters To A Daughter,* was often attended by the impression that here is a 19th century Solomon intent upon imparting to his child a wisdom and sanctified common sense akin to The Proverbs. Indeed, as one familiar with The Proverbs reads this volume, repeated connections will be readily made between the practical directives it contains and the inspired wisdom set before Solomon's son.

To an age which exhibits a lamentable and gravely deficient performance of parental responsibilities, this collection of fatherly letters is a rebuke. Portrayed throughout these addresses on practical subjects is a caring father exercising an active, intelligent and far-sighted parental leadership which is in stunning contrast to the passivity and thoughtlessness which characterizes parenthood today. Further, to a generation wherein parents transmit to their children values and lifestyle geared to the present moment and the gratification of the present impulse, W. B. Sprague's, *Letters,* reflect the biblical perspective of the transcending worth of the soul. Regardless of the particular subject address, this father evidences the conscious awareness that his daughter's greatest good can be realized only in saving union with Christ and that her surpassing duty in this life is to work out her salvation by cultivating the graces and virtues of Christian character. The certainties of death and judgment seem never to be far from this father's mind whether he counsels his daughter on the formation of friendships or practical religion.

While the counsel of this book is applicable to sons as well as daughters, arresting throughout was the recognition that the reader not only benefits from the spirit-wrought wisdom conveyed on its pages but also from the skillful and exemplary relationship of a mature masculinity with a developing femininity. Rearing godly offspring is a demanding task for the most conscientious of parents. Such a task takes on even more formidable dimensions when it embraces a father-daughter relationship. The temperamental, constitutional and role differences which distinguish and define manhood and womanhood require consummate wisdom on the part of a father if he is to guide his daughter into the possession of a godly femininity. W. B. Sprague's example and counsel should hearten and assist any father in the task.

George McDearmon
Ballston Lake Baptist Church
Ballston Lake, New York
1987

PREFACE.

THE following letters were originally designed to be preserved in manuscript, as a leg-
acy to a motherless child. The circumstances
which have resulted in their being given to the
world it is unnecessary to state. It has been
the design of the writer to adapt the work, in
its present form, to the various exigencies of a
young female, and to furnish her with counsel
and instruction which may be useful, not only
during the period of her education, but also in
subsequent life. Though the letters are addressed to his own child, he regards her as the
representative of young females in general; and
his object in writing them will be fully answered
if they shall contribute, in the humblest degree,
to elevate the standard of female acquisitions
and female character. The author has only to

add his earnest prayer that they may be read with some degree of advantage by young females into whose hands they may fall; and especially by those whom the righteous providence of God has deprived of the benefit of maternal care and instruction.

LETTERS

ON

PRACTICAL SUBJECTS.

LETTER I.

INTRODUCTORY.

My DEAR CHILD—It is for the heart of the parent alone, adequately to conceive of the tender responsibilities that belong to the parental relation. It is impossible, if he have the feelings of a man—much more of a Christian—that he should contemplate a beloved child coming forward into life, and beginning a career for eternity, without agitating in his own bosom the question, what the probable condition of that child may be in the future stages of existence. And, if I mistake not, there are some special reasons why the solicitude of a parent should be awakened by contemplating the condition of a *daughter* during the critical period to which I have referred. In addition to all the other circumstances which render her an object of deep interest, and in which she shares in common with children of the other sex, she is, in a higher degree than they, dependent on parental aid : there is a sort of natural defencelessness in her condition, independently of the fostering care of those from whom, under God, she received her being, that makes an appeal to a parent's heart, which, if it be not a heart of stone, he will strive in vain to resist.

If I should say that the common feelings of parental solicitude have something to do in dictating the plan of addressing the following letters to you, I should certainly tell you the truth, but not the whole truth ; for your circumstances, though by no means peculiar to yourself, have been preëminently fitted to give you a high place not only in the affections, but the sympathies of your father. It was my lot, in the wise but mysterious providence of God, to see your mother taken from you at an age when you were incapable of estimating her affection or your loss ; and to find myself at the same moment looking for the last time on the cold remains of a beloved wife, and listening to the unconscious but piercing cries of a motherless child. While I shall always remember that moment with emotions not to be told, I can never fail to connect with it a recollection of the goodness of God in ordering so favorably the circumstances of your infancy,

and in giving you, in due time, another mother, who
counts it a privilege to do her utmost to make you
good and useful and happy. You will instantly perceive that the circumstances to which I have now
adverted, could hardly fail to awaken a deep and
permanent interest in a father's heart; and I assure
you they have had much to do in bringing me to the
resolution to write the following letters.

That you may be the better prepared to estimate
the importance of the various topics to which I intend,
in these letters, to direct your attention, I beg you to
remember that what you are at the age of eighteen or
twenty, you probably will be, making due allowance
for the change of circumstances, in every future period
of life. In other words, your character will by that
time, in all probability, have acquired a fixed direction—
a direction which will last through all the scenes of
your prosperity and adversity to your dying hour;
which will influence and control all your prospects as
it respects comfort, respectability, and usefulness here;
and which will go farther, and shed upon your prospects for a future world the brightness of immortal
glory, or the blackness of endless despair. I admit
that there are many exceptions from this remark; but
I appeal to the records of human experience, I appeal
to the observation of any individual who has been
accustomed carefully to notice facts on this subject,
whether the general truth be not as above stated:
that in the great majority of cases, the character of

a young female, at the close of her education, is formed for life—of course, formed for eternity. I am sure this consideration cannot fail, if you duly estimate it, to give deep interest to every effort, and especially every parental effort, that is made to lead you to virtue and happiness.

I am aware that much has been written on the subjects upon which I am to address you, and with a degree of ability to which I can make no claim. Nevertheless, I am constrained to say that most of the books with which I am acquainted, designed for the special benefit of young females, have seemed to me either deficient in some important topics of instruction, or to contain views on some other points from which an intelligent Christian parent would be compelled to dissent. Far be it from me to intimate that I expect in these letters to supply all the deficiencies, or correct all the mistakes, of those who have gone before me: I only promise that the views which I communicate shall be such as, after mature reflection, and I trust I may add, earnest prayer, appear to me to be consonant with reason, experience, and Scripture. I have no ambition to say any thing that shall appear new or striking, but my whole object is to give you plain parental advice on topics which do not lose their importance with their novelty. And it is a thought upon which I dwell with some interest, that though you might read the writings of a stranger with indifference, you will peruse these letters with attention and perhaps advantage, when the heart that dictates them shall have ceased to beat, and the hand by which they are penned shall have mouldered into dust.

I hardly need tell you that my first wish and most fervent prayer on your behalf is, that you may *remember your Creator in the days of your youth.* Unless you embrace the gospel as a redeeming and purifying system—in other words, unless you become a practical follower of the Lord Jesus Christ, it would profit you nothing in the end, though you should have every other accomplishment which can adorn your character or recommend you to the world. In the progress of these letters, I shall dwell on the subject of practical religion with some degree of particularity ; and I wish you distinctly to remember, while I am directing your attention to other subjects, that they are all subordinate to this. To see you walking in the truth and keeping the commandments of God, will, more than any thing else, gladden the heart of

Your affectionate

FATHER.

LETTER II.

EARLY FRIENDSHIPS.

MY DEAR CHILD—The development of the social principle is one of the earliest exhibitions of human nature.   This, in connection with the benevolent affections, constitutes the foundation of friendship.   Hence we find that strong attachments often exist between children, long before the judgment is sufficiently developed to decide in respect to the qualities which should enter into the character of a friend.   A glance at your own short experience will convince you that it has been conformed to this law of our condition. You will find on a review of your childhood, that you have formed many friendships without much discrimination, some of which may have already given place to others ; while some, perhaps, may continue to the evening of life.

The importance of early friendships is to be estimated by the influence which they exert in forming the character.   That this influence must be very great, no one can question who has considered either the constitution of our nature, or the actual results which are found in experience.   We are originally constituted creatures of habit, subject, in a high degree, to the influence of example; and though many of the impressions which the mind receives in childhood are necessarily worn out in its progress to maturity, yet those which remain are wrought into the very texture of the character, and become the most efficient principles of action. Every person who attentively examines his own character, or who is intimately acquainted with the process by which the characters of others have been formed, will find sufficient proof of the reality and extent of this influence. Who has not heard, on witnessing the wreck of parental hopes in a ruined and wretched child, that it was the melancholy result of bad early associations? And who, on the other hand, has not watched with delight the benign influence of a virtuous friendship upon the unfolding faculties of the mind and dispositions of the heart?

If so much importance be attached to the friendships which you form in early life, you will at once perceive that the choice of your friends ought to be a matter of the most deliberate caution; for though your earliest attachments must necessarily result from circumstances not within your control, yet, in respect to those which are formed subsequently to the period of childhood, you may call to your aid judgment and reflection. A rule on this subject which you should never fail to observe is, not too hastily to proffer your confidence—not to consent to an unreserved intimacy with any one, till you have gained a thorough knowledge of the character. The effect of disregarding this rule would be, to lower the estimate which would be formed of your friendship, to expose you, at least, to the charge of imprudence, and not improbably, to many more serious evils. You may safely calculate that considerable suspicion is to be attached to professions which are made by those who have had little opportunity to know you; while you may reasonably expect, on the other hand, that a friendship which is the result of an intimate acquaintance, will be a lasting source of pleasure and advantage.

In respect to the character of your particular friends, I hardly need say that you are not to expect to find those who are free from imperfection or sin. You will recollect that in common with yourself, they belong to a race of fallen beings; and it would be strange indeed, if there should not be occasion, both on your part and theirs, for mutual condescension to each other's infirmities, and mutual forgiveness of each other's errors. Nevertheless, in the selection of your friends, you may safely place your standard as high as is consistent with our present fallen state; and you ought, in no case, unnecessarily to contract an intimate friendship with one whose example, on the whole, you would not choose to imitate; for this obvious reason, that the tendency of such a friendship to assimilate its subjects is so strong, that there is little probability, in any given case, of its being counteracted.

One quality which is of great importance in an

intimate friend, is an amiable temper. Every one knows how much of the unhappiness of life results from the haughty, irritable, and unkind feelings of those with whom we are even remotely associated ; of course, the evil becomes greater in proportion to the nearness of the relation which we sustain to them. A person of an unamiable temper was never formed either to enjoy or impart the highest pleasure connected with friendship ; for though one of this character may be sincerely attached to you, and may be, on the whole, quite desirous of promoting your happiness, it would be passing strange if your intercourse with her should not frequently be imbittered by hasty or unkind expressions. I advise you therefore, in the selection of your friends, to have particular reference to the natural disposition ; and as a general rule, not to admit to your unreserved confidence any who would be likely often to wound your sensibility, and whose feelings are not, and cannot be attuned to the enjoyments of a refined friendship.

Another trait which it is desirable that your intimate friends should possess, is a good and cultivated understanding. I do not mean that you are to consider it indispensably requisite that a friend should be possessed of uncommon genius, or should have made great attainments in any of the departments of science or literature ; but there is a wide difference between the accomplishments of which I now speak, which fall to the lot of comparatively few, and that intellectual barrenness which must oppose an effectual barrier to all pleasant or useful intercourse. One important purpose which you ought to propose to yourself in an intimate friendship, is the culture of the understanding ; for besides the advantages for improvement which are connected with an unreserved intercourse, it would be obviously wrong that so much time as that intercourse would probably occupy, should be spent without contributing in any degree to the strength or development of the intellectual faculties. If your most intimate associates are persons of good sense and a good degree of improvement, you can hardly fail to derive some intellectual advantage from mingling in their society ; you will breathe an atmosphere which will operate almost insensibly to invigorate the powers of your mind. But if, on the other hand, you are most conversant with those whose minds are cast in an inferior mould, and whose opportunities of mental cultivation are very narrow, you will not only lose much positive advantage, but it will be strange if your own mind does not gradually come to sympathize in the imbecility and barrenness with which it is so constantly brought in contact.

As another quality which you ought to regard in the choice of your friends, I would mention discretion. This is something quite distinct · from genius, but though a less dazzling quality, it is probably more important both to happiness and usefulness. Many a female of a brilliant and cultivated mind has sacrificed her own character and the comfort of her friends to indiscretion. If your most intimate friends are of this character, the evil to yourself will be twofold : you will partake of the unhappiness which they will frequently bring upon themselves, and you will often yourself be subject to embarrassment and perplexity in consequence of their imprudence. Never be attracted then, in the selection of a friend, by any appearance of eccentricity. In almost every case, you will find it associated with some kind of indiscretion ; and wherever this exists in any considerable degree, it will be enough to poison the most intimate friendship. Let your friends be those who have the reputation of being prudent and judicious. Better that they should possess these qualities than every artificial accomplishment.

I will only add in respect to the character of your particular friends, that it is exceedingly desirable that they should be persons who maintain a serious regard for religion, and who live under its practical influence. In the formation of your friendships as well as in every thing else, you are to recollect that you are an immortal and accountable creature, and to keep in view your preparation for a future world. Nothing will serve more effectually to prevent or banish all serious impressions, than an unrestrained intercourse with the vain and careless. Whatever other attractions such persons may possess, you may rest assured that the single fact that they treat religion with levity or

indifference, is a sufficient reason why they snould not
be your chosen friends. Indeed, the more .engaging
they are in other respects, the more reason would you
have to dread their influence as companions, because
they would throw around an irreligious life so many
more dangerous attractions. Let your intimate friends,
therefore, be at least persons who pay a conscientious
regard to the duties of religion ; and if they have
deeply felt its power, you ought to regard it as an
additional recommendation. If you rightly improve
the privilege, you will not have occasion at the close
of life, to lament that your most intimate associates
were persons of exemplary piety. But if you should
choose friends of an opposite character, you have great
reason to fear that the remembrance of it will imbitter
your closing hour with unavailing regrets.

Let me here remark, as a direction which you will
do well always to keep in mind, that your particular
friends should not be very numerous. My reasons for
this advice are the following. To meet all the claims
which many intimate friendships would involve, would
require too much of your time, and would necessarily
interfere with the duties connected with your station
in life. You could derive no advantage from having
many intimate friends, which would not be as well
secured to you by a smaller circle ; and indeed, just in
proportion as the number is extended beyond a moderate limit, you will defeat the purposes which such a
friendship is designed to answer. For it is impossible,

from the nature of the case, that you should bestow the same degree of confidence and affection upon a great number as upon a few ; and as the advantage to be derived is, in some measure, in proportion to the strength and intimacy of the friendship, it is obvious that the more numerous is your circle of particular friends, the less satisfaction and benefit you can expect to receive. It is equally true, on the other hand, that the greater the number to whom you proffer your confidence, the less will your confidence be valued in each particular case ; for there is no exception here from the general rule, that things are cheap in proportion as they are common. Be satisfied then with a few choice friends, and be not ambitious to be the confidant of all your acquaintance.

Another suggestion closely connected with the one which I have just made, is, that you should not be fickle in your friendships—not hastily give up one friend for the sake of gaining another. Wherever this disposition is discovered, it is sure to excite disgust, and to attach suspicion to any subsequent professions. Be as cautious as you will in forming your attachments, but when they are once formed, never let them be broken unless on some ground that you can justify to your reason and conscience. One single instance of the unreasonable desertion of a friend would do an injury to your character which time could scarcely wear out, or future fidelity retrieve.

It only remains that I suggest a few hints in respect

to the manner in which your intercourse with your
friends should be regulated. That you should treat
them with a high degree of confidence is implied in
the fact that you extend to them a particular friendship. Never wound them by any unreasonable expressions of distrust, or by withholding from them any
thing which they have a right to know. Be particularly cautious not to excite curiosity by dropping a
hint in relation to subjects which, from any consideration, you do not feel willing fully to explain. Such
mysterious allusions often excite painful suspicions in
the mind, and have not unfrequently been instrumental
in separating chief friends. It would be too paltry a
consideration for which to wound the feelings, or to
expose yourself to the loss, of a valued friend, that you
might be amused by witnessing the common operations
of curiosity.

But while I would have you as unreserved in your
intercourse with your friends as the relation which you
bear to them demands, I would also have you beware
of the opposite extreme of pouring into their ears
every thing which you may happen to know, without
discrimination. In your intercourse with a censorious
world, it would be strange if you should not sometimes
hear remarks upon their characters which, however
unmeaning in themselves, could not be repeated in
their hearing without giving pain. Make it a rule,
therefore, never to carry any unfavorable report to a
friend, unless you believe that it will in some way or

other be productive of good. Not a small part of the
ill rumors which exist in society are to be traced to a
habit of gossiping, rather than to any settled purpose
to slander; and if you should carry every thing of
this kind that you hear to your friends to whom it relates, no doubt they would often be severely wounded,
where there was no positive intention of attacking
their character.

I would say, too, that in your intercourse with each
of your friends, you ought to maintain a scrupulous
reserve in respect to what may have been confiden-
tially intrusted to you by others. Your duty requires
that you should pay a sacred regard to the confidence
which each reposes in you; and none of them can
reasonably claim that you should betray another for
their gratification. If you have several intimate
friends who are not at the same time the intimate
friends of each other, you should bear in mind, that in
disclosing to one a secret which has been committed
to you by another, you violate a fundamental principle
of good friendship; for however you may confide in
the prudence and good faith of the person to whom
you make the disclosure, you obviously assume a right
which does not belong to you—that of giving notoriety
to the private concerns of an individual beyond what
you have reason to believe were her intentions and
wishes. And the case is not materially different in
this respect, even where the friend who confides a
secret to you, and the friend to whom you confide the

same, are intimate with each other: there might be
many reasons which would render it desirable that it
should not be known to a third person, however
friendly, which might not exist in respect to yourself;
and at any rate, your friend does not feel, and ought
not to feel, when she intrusts a private concern to
your keeping, in which perhaps she alone is interested,
that she thereby relinquishes the privilege of deciding
whether or not it is to be communicated to others.
You will therefore consider the secrets of each one of
your friends as a separate and independent trust, which
you are faithfully and sacredly to regard.

There is one duty of great delicacy, to which you
may sometimes be called in your intercourse with
your friends—I mean, that of reproof or admonition.
Though I have advised you to set your standard high
in selecting your intimate associates, and to choose
those whom you believe to be the best models of
character, you will not be disappointed to find them
sometimes in the wrong; nor ought you to make every
foible which you may notice in them the subject of
animadversion.   At the same time it admits of no
question, that occasions may arise which will not only
warrant, but imperatively demand, that you should
take the attitude of a reprover; and on which to remain silent, would be a gross violation of the obligations of friendship.   There was a mutual pledge virtually given when your friendship was formed, that you
would sacredly endeavor to promote each other's best

interests; and you surely do not redeem this pledge, if you suffer gross errors to pass unreproved. The great secret of discharging this duty successfully, is to choose a proper time and place, and to do it in the spirit of gentleness and affection. Whenever you take this attitude, instead of appearing to have thrown off the character of a friend, and assuming an air of cold severity, you should let every expression and look testify that you are, if possible, more under the influence of genuine friendship than ever. If you only succeed in making an impression that the reproof is the honest dictate of true kindness, you will be in little danger of failing of your object; but if unhappily you leave the impression that it proceeded from personal irritation, or from an unreasonable misconstruction of your conduct, it would be strange indeed if you should realize a happy result.

In general, I would say that you ought to make all· your intercourse with your friends as profitable as you can, both to yourself and them. It is hardly possible but that the friendships which you form should be to you a source of great good, or great evil. If the time which you spend with your intimate associates is chiefly devoted, as it should be, to the improvement of the intellect and the heart, you will never review it but with feelings of approbation. But if, on the other hand, it is given to levity and vanity, and if those whom you regard with most affection are coworkers with you in murdering the hours which were given for better purposes, then you have reason to expect that the friendships which you now form, instead of being the channel of blessings, will serve to poison your moral sentiments, and to accumulate anguish for a dying hour.

Your affectionate

FATHER.

LETTER III.

EDUCATION — GENERAL DIRECTIONS.

My DEAR CHILD—In this and some following letters, I design to give you my views briefly on the subject of education. I say *briefly*, for the subject is of such extent, and has so many important connections, that one could scarcely think of doing justice to it in any thing short of an extended treatise. I shall confine myself to such hints as I think may be most useful to you in prosecuting your own education.

I would have you, then, in the first place, bear in mind that the great object of your education is to enable you to bring into exercise the powers which God has given you in such a manner as shall contribute most to his glory. For all the noble faculties with which you are gifted, you are indebted to the same Being who gave you your existence: on Him also you are dependent for their preservation ; and it is a first dictate of reason that they should be employed in his service. But these faculties are evidently susceptible of high cultivation ; and without it they can never accomplish the purpose for which they are designed. The object of education then is twofold : to develope the faculties and to direct them ; to bring out the energies of the soul, and to bring them to operate to the glory of the Creator. In other words, it is to render you useful to the extent of your ability.

From this view of the design of education in general, it would seem that no one, certainly no Christian, could dissent. But who does not know that in the education of females, even this fundamental principle has too often been overlooked ; and that too by parents who have professed to regulate their whole conduct by a regard to Christian obligation? Especially has this capital error been committed in substituting what is called an ornamental, for a solid education—in taking more care to form the person than to form the mind ; and the consequence of this has been, that many a girl of fine natural talents has come forth to the world and shown us the fruit of a long and expensive education, in the marvellous dexterity she has acquired in the use of her hands and feet. But are not females gifted with the exalted attribute of reason as well as the other sex? And where has Providence intimated that in one sex this gift is to be cultivated with the utmost care, and in the other is to be left in all the wildness and barrenness of nature? What if the sexes have not, in all respects, the same destination? What if man is destined to stand forth in the bolder walks of society ; and what if woman has her station

allotted her more exclusively amidst the retired scenes
of domestic life? This may be a reason why their education should in some respects be differently conducted;
but it can never be an argument for leaving the mind
of the female to rust with ignorance, or moulding her
into a pleasant, animated plaything. If it be desirable
that the mind of man should expand and strengthen
by exercise, it must also be desirable that the female
mind should share in some degree the same cultivation:
otherwise the dearest, tenderest connection of life,
which ought to be but another name for the most absolute community of interest and feeling, will be con-
verted into an unequal, unnatural league between intellectual refinement and intellectual barbarism.

You perceive then that the object of female education cannot be attained without careful attention to
the culture of the intellect. And let me say that this
must extend to the intellect in all its powers—to the
perception, the judgment, the memory, the reasoning
faculty, etc. This is important, not only because each
of these various faculties has its distinct office, and
just in proportion as it is suffered to remain dormant
or turned out of its proper direction, the end for which
it is designed is defeated; but because the different
faculties have a mutual dependence upon each other,
and like the parts of a well-adjusted machine, operate
most legitimately and most effectually where the balance is carefully preserved. It is true indeed, that
much respect should be paid to the peculiar constitu-

tion of the mind ; and it should be trained to put forth its most commanding efforts by means of its strongest powers : nevertheless, there are none of your faculties which you have a right to neglect; and even the feeblest of them should be cultivated, at least so far that the mind may attain its fair and just proportion.

It is also desirable, in order that you may attain the true end of education, that you should, as far as possible, adopt a course which will combine particular and general utility ; that is, the various branches which you pursue should be such as may be turned to some practical use, while they minister to the general culture of the mind, and give it the easy command of its own powers. The most interesting view of the education of the mind is that which regards it as a system designed to bring out its powers and carry it forward from one degree of strength to another. What though you may gain ever so much knowledge, if every new degree of it is not a new degree of intellectual power you do not reap the legitimate fruit of your mental toil. That this important object may be gained, accustom yourself in every branch of study to independent reflection, and let your mind freely think its own thoughts, and be not afraid to presume that the text-book itself, where it is any thing else than the Bible, may be wrong. Not that I would encourage in you a habit of intellectual presumption : that in any youth were disgusting—in a young female it were intolerable. But that habit of modest inquisitiveness which asks

for a reason for whatever it assents to, and which un-
ostentatiously pushes its inquiries beyond authority, or
even in the face of authority, is always to be commended ; and is fitted above almost any other habit
of mind to give you a knowledge of your powers on
the one hand, and a command of them on the other.

Let me here say a word in regard to the use and
abuse of text-books.   That you may derive from them
important aid in the prosecution of your studies, there
can be no doubt ; and there is as little question that
they are capable of being perverted as auxiliaries to
mental inaction.   The true use to be made of them is,
not to supersede, but to assist reflection ; not merely
to communicate information, but to give an impulse
to the intellect, by suggesting hints and principles
which it may follow out to their legitimate results.
But the danger is, that while your memory will be laid
under contribution to gather up whatever is said in
the text-book, your other faculties will find a ready
dispensation ; and that in your recitation you will be
satisfied to confine yourself to the very letter of your
author.   In order to guard against this evil, let what
is said in the text-book be regarded as only the basis
of what you are to learn ; and let it serve as a guide
to conduct you into other fields of thought ; and accustom yourself to scrutinize every principle, and seek
for a solution of every difficulty that may present
itself.   Such a use of text-books, while it will not expose your mind to be enslaved by authorities, or leave

any of its faculties to rust through inaction, will secure every positive advantage which a record of the labors of other minds can impart.

But while you should keep in view the general culture of your mind, it is important that each particular branch that you pursue should be of practical utility. It cannot be denied that the intellectual labors of many of the schoolmen, previous to the revival of learning in Europe, were of great extent, and were fitted to produce a high degree of mental acumen. But every one who has looked into their writings knows that the subjects upon which they employed their faculties were of little practical moment; and that, they would often pour out a world of learned nonsense to establish a point, which after all was not worth establishing. They indeed, by this means, acquired an extraordinary power of discrimination; and this the true theory of education certainly does not overlook; but it aims at this end by employing the mind upon subjects of practical utility—subjects which it can turn to some account in the every-day affairs of life. And let me say that it is important not only that the knowledge which you acquire should be practical, but that you should also gain the ability of carrying it out, as you may have opportunity, in the various departments of human action. You might have every variety of learning, and if withal you had not learned to reduce it to practise, you could never rise above an educated dunce; whereas a much less degree of knowledge, with the ability of applying it, would render you at once respectable and useful.

I have cautioned you against an improper reliance on text-books : it is equally important that you should guard against depending too much on instructors. Why is it that many a girl of good natural talents, after enjoying the best advantages of education for years, comes away from school a mere smatterer in most branches included in her course, and thoroughly versed in none ? The reason often is, that she has contented herself with being in a literary atmosphere, and going through the daily routine of recitations ; and while she has depended upon her instructor to solve every difficulty, has hardly taxed herself with the labor of so much thought as was necessary to apprehend his explanations. Now I wish you to be deeply impressed with the truth, that all the instruction in the world will never make you a scholar independently of your own efforts. There is no such thing as thinking by proxy, any more than breathing by proxy : intellectual acquisitions must be the fruit of intellectual labor ; and whoever will not encounter the one, must be satisfied to remain destitute of the other. I say then, listen attentively to all that is communicated by your instructors, and endeavor to make the best use of it ; but that this may be the case,. let their thoughts become incorporated with your own, just as you do, or as you ought to do, in relation to the thoughts of the authors whom you study. Your

instructors may indeed coöperate with you in the cultivation of your mind; but if you undertake to throw
the whole burden upon them, the result may indeed
witness to their fidelity, but it certainly will witness
to your folly and mortification.

Closely connected with the faithful exercise of your
own faculties, independently of text-books and teachers, is a habit of diligence. I do not mean that your
whole time is to be occupied in study; this, while it
would expose your health, would impair the vigor of
your faculties, and thus diminish your amount of acquisition. I would have you exercise your mind closely
in study when you exercise it at all; and exercise it
as constantly as is consistent with keeping it in the
best state for successful application. While you profess to be a student, regard study as your main business; and make your amusement subordinate, and, so
far as possible, subservient to it. Recollect that the
period allotted to your education is comparatively
short; and that every wasted hour of this golden
season will tell fearfully on your future destiny.

I have just alluded to the fact—and I wish here to
bring it more distinctly before you—that in order that
you may study to the most advantage, part of your
time must be devoted to relaxation and exercise; how
large a part, your own judgment and experience must
decide. Many a young female of great promise has
laid the foundation of disease that has carried her prematurely to the grave, by neglecting bodily exercise

during the period of her education. And not only has she sacrificed her life to this unfortunate habit, but her intellectual acquisitions have actually been less than if a due proportion of her time had been devoted to the exercise of her bodily powers. Whether, therefore, you regard the preservation of your life and health, or your success in the various branches of study, I earnestly entreat you to subject yourself to a course of daily, systematic exercise. In following this advice you will be surprised to find how much you will gain in respect to elasticity of spirits and vigor of thought; and that you will often accomplish more mental labor in a single hour, than under other circumstances you would accomplish in a day, or even a week. And more than this, instead of leaving school with a constitution whose resources are more than half exhausted, and with an ominous paleness on your cheek, which seems to say that the grave is ready for you, you will probably come away in the bloom of health, and with strength and resolution to engage in the duties of the station in which Providence may place you.

Let me say a word in this connection in regard to the treatment which is due from you to your instructors. Next to your parents, your instructors, if they are faithful, are most actively engaged in the formation of your character, and they watch over you with a degree of solicitude inferior only to that which belongs to the parental relation. It is obvious, therefore, that not only common propriety but gratitude requires that

you should treat them with great deference and respect.
You are not indeed bound to receive every or any
opinion they may express without examination; and
you are at liberty, unless for particular reasons they
should choose to forbid it, modestly to propose difficulties which may be suggestèd even by their own
instruction; but you are always faithfully to consult
their wishes, and yield a ready obedience to their
requisitions, and by your kind and respectful deportment, to do what you can to diminish the burden of
care and perplexity that is inseparable from their employment. I should do you injustice to suppose it
possible that you should be guilty of such indecorum
as deliberately to trifle with the feelings of your instructors, or incur their open and direct censure; but
your conduct towards them would never satisfy me,
unless it should be such as to secure their positive and
uniform approbation.

I cannot close this letter without again reminding
you that, as an accountable and immortal creature,
you are to regard all other kinds of improvement as
subordinate to the culture of the heart; and that your
acquisitions, if they are not sanctified by divine grace,
will ultimately prove a curse to you rather than a
blessing. While I am earnestly desirous that you
should make the most of your opportunities for improving your mind, I confess that I am not without
apprehension lest you should neglect the one thing
needful; and more than that, lest you should find

temptations to the neglect of it growing out of circumstances connected with your education. If you have
a strong relish for study, there is danger that study
will become with you the all-engrossing concern, and
will leave you without any thoughts to bestow upon
God or your soul's salvation. There is danger too,
that in your daily and accidental intercourse with
thoughtless companions, you will contract the same
habit of indifference to religion which you witness in
them, and this habit will soon become fortified by the
powerful influence of example, and the dread of being
singular. Such has been the melancholy result in relation to many a young female, who has commenced
her education not only under the influence of pious
parental precepts and counsels, but with a tender conscience, with a habit of serious reflection, and with
strong resolutions for entering on the religious life.
You cannot wonder then that I am desirous to apprize
you of these temptations, and to urge you to be on
your guard against them. And that you may resist
them effectually, let me counsel you to let a portion of
each day be sacredly devoted to meditation upon your
character and condition as a sinful and immortal being,
to the attentive perusal of the holy Scriptures, and to
earnest endeavors for the sanctifying influences of the
Holy Spirit. In a word, let me entreat you to become
a new creature in Christ Jesus—a practical and decided Christian. This will not only save you from the
danger of being fatally ensnared by thoughtless asso-

ciates, but it will impart to your example a dignity
and loveliness and power, which, under God, may render you instrumental of their salvation.   It will at
once secure to you the largest amount of intellectual
improvement, and will be a pledge that all your acquisitions will be consecrated to the best interests of
your fellow-creatures, and to the honor of your Creator
and Redeemer.

Your affectionate

FATHER.

LETTER IV.

EDUCATION — VARIOUS BRANCHES.

My DEAR CHILD—Having, in a preceding letter, called your attention to some general views of the subject of education, I design in this, to enumerate some of the various branches which will naturally be included in your course, and to give you my opinion of their comparative importance. Whatever relates to the selection and order of your studies, I am willing to leave in a great measure to your instructors, not doubting that they will direct you with good judgment; and I am willing too to leave something to your own taste and inclination; but as this is a subject which deeply involves the improvement of your mind and the formation of your character, and in which a father must of course feel a deep interest, you will not wonder that I am disposed to give you briefly the result of my experience and reflection.

You need not be startled, when I go back to the very elementary branches of an education, and begin

to talk to you on the simple matter of learning to read.
That you can read with tolerable correctness and some
degree of fluency already, I admit; but you have at
least as much to learn as you have learned already,
before you can be, in any proper sense of the phrase,
a good reader. My first advice is, that you should
adopt in every respect the tones of nature—the tones
which you are accustomed to use in common conversation. Almost every child contracts, at a very early
period, what is commonly called a reading tone—a
monotonous habit of utterance, which, while it out-
rages taste and nature, is generally with great difficulty broken up. If you have already contracted this
tone in any degree—and it would be strange indeed if
you had not—make it your first object to get rid of it.
When you sit down to read, do not think it necessary
to assume a more formal or stately mental attitude,
than if you were sitting down to converse; and endeavor to utter the sentiments of your author in *his*
language, in the same easy and familiar manner that
you would talk off the same sentiments in your own.
This of course implies that you read intelligently—
that you are able to enter into the spirit of your
author, and readily and fully to apprehend his meaning. You can never attain what I wish in this respect
by the study of rules, though these may be of some
assistance to you: you can only do it by understanding well what you read, and giving yourself up to the
simple dictate of nature; and by often-repeated exer-

cises of this kind, you will acquire the habit which I am recommending. Be careful also that you utter each sentence, and every part of each sentence, with perfect distinctness, and in so loud a tone that all that you say shall not only be heard, but heard without effort. Guard, on the one hand, against fatiguing the attention of those who listen to you, by the excessive rapidity of your utterance, and on the other, against furnishing them with an apology for going to sleep by your extreme deliberation. In a word, let it be your aim to read in such a manner as most deeply to impress the sentiments of your author, and of course, most effectually to secure the attention of your hearers.

Next to reading comes the equally simple art of spelling. It is true of this as of every other elementary branch, and if I mistake not, in a higher degree than of any other, that if it is not learned at a very early period, it will probably never be learned at all; and hence it is not uncommon to find men, whose early education was neglected, but who, by their own subsequent exertions, have risen to the most elevated stations, leaving evidence through life upon every thing they write that they do not understand the art of making words out of letters. This indeed may be excused where there has been the want of early advantages; but nothing else can render it tolerable. I beg you will make it a point, therefore, as early as possible, to possess yourself of a correct system of orthography. This is a thing to be learned partly by rule, but in a much greater degree, by practice ; and without much of the latter, I assure you that you can never arrive at much perfection in this simple but necessary department of knowledge. Let me advise you in writing never to run the hazard of committing an orthographical error, in a case in respect to which you are in doubt. Always settle the point on the spot, where it is practicable, by a reference to some standard authority. In this way you will acquire a habit of correctness, and a particularity of information, which will soon make you independent of dictionaries ; whereas, by adopting the opposite course, you will not only run the hazard of committing an error, in a case in which an error, to say the least, is hardly decent, but you will acquire a habit of inattention to your orthography which may ultimately make it a task for a literary friend to read your composition.

As for penmanship, I cannot say that I regard it so important that you should attain to high excellence in it, as in either of the preceding branches ; and yet I am desirous that your attainments in this department should, at least, be respectable. I should be glad to see you write an easy and graceful hand, and above all, I would have it possess the attribute of being legible. A more odd conceit never entered a human head than seems to have gotten possession of some at the present day—that a hand which puts one's invention to the torture, is a sure mark of genius. If that be the test, I will only say that I choose to have you run the hazard of being considered a dunce, rather than torment me and your other friends with illegible communications. How much truth there is in the doctrine held by some, that the handwriting indicates the intellectual or moral character, I will not undertake to decide; but I earnestly hope that you will take up no doctrine or practice on this subject that will prevent you from being a neat, plain, and if you please, elegant writer.

I hardly need say that you can lay no claim to the character of an accomplished scholar, until you can speak and write with correctness your own language. And in order for this, you must gain a thorough knowledge of English grammar and rhetoric. These branches should be so familiar to you, that you will, as a matter of course, and without even being conscious of it at the time, judge every composition you read or hear by grammatical or rhetorical rules; that you will as instantly detect an error in syntax or an error in taste, as a delicate ear would notice a confusion in musical sounds. I know indeed there have been those who have written with great power, and even beauty, who have known nothing of rhetoric or grammar, except as they were taught by nature—whose minds would pour out "thoughts that breathe in words that burn," with the same apparent ease that a stream flows from its fountain; but there is no reason to doubt that even these preëminently gifted individuals would have done better with the know-

ledge of which I am speaking, than they did without
it ; and at any rate, they are exceptions from a general
rule, and therefore furnish no ground for any general
conclusion.

It were hardly necessary to say that a habit of easy
and elegant composition is not to be acquired in ordinary cases without much attention and long continued
practice.   If you should find, therefore, that your first
efforts are rather tame and feeble, it will be no reason
why you should be discouraged ; for no doubt there
are many now on the list of fine writers whose first
efforts were as tame and feeble as yours.   Nothing
will serve more effectually to improve your taste, and
to give you an easy command of thought and expression, than an intimate acquaintance with the English
classics.   You will also, especially in your earlier es-
says at composition, find it a useful exercise, after you
lay aside your book, to commit the thoughts of your
author to paper in your own language ; though I
hardly need say that you are never to attempt to pass
off any thing that you produce in this way as your
own, in any higher sense than it actually is so ; for to
say nothing of the immorality of such an act, which I
should hope would be sufficient to deter you from it,
there is no character in the literary world regarded
with more odium than a plagiarist.   Remember, that
to form a good writer, the first requisite is good
thoughts—the second, a good style.   If you can command thoughts which are striking and original, it is

all the better, provided they are appropriate; but endeavor always to be appropriate at any rate. A striking thought introduced merely because it *is* striking, and with nothing in the connection to justify it, is a blemish, and not an ornament; an indication both of the lack of judgment and of taste. Whenever you have selected your subject, and have possessed yourself of the necessary information in respect to it, revolve it thoroughly in your mind, and see what appropriately belongs to it; and then select such thoughts or trains of thought as may seem to you on the whole most pertinent and useful. Arrange your thoughts, so far as may be, before you begin to write; and then you will proceed with far more ease, and probably with far more success. Let your subjects be chosen, so far as possible, with reference to the general culture of your mind. It is too much the fashion of the day for girls, in writing their compositions, to imagine themselves surveying some beautiful moonlight scene, or listening to the sound of some magnificent cataract, or contemplating nature in some other of her wild or sweet or majestic forms: all this may be well enough for an occasional exercise of imagination; but in general I advise you to select subjects of more practical interest— subjects which are adapted to exercise the judgment, the reasoning faculty, and other powers of the mind, and not merely to awaken or improve the fancy. The secret of forming a good style is to throw into it a due proportion of gracefulness and strength. There are a thousand good models which I might recommend to you, but I am not desirous that you should closely study any model as such ; the true mode is, to be conversant with as many good writers as you can, and to let your mind operate in its own way, unembarrassed by the peculiarities of any. I am always delighted to read a book on which I can see the very image and superscription of the author's own mind.

Of the various kinds of composition there is none perhaps to which young females generally are more inclined, and for which they find more occasion, than the epistolary ; and I must do your sex the justice to say that in this respect they greatly exceed ours under the same advantages. Without saying any thing here of the propriety of your cultivating a more extensive or a more limited correspondence, I would urge upon you the importance of acquiring a good epistolary style, for this, among other reasons, that it is an accomplishment which is well fitted to make you agreeable to your friends. And the only particular direction which I would give you for acquiring it, supposing you to be attentive to the general culture of your mind, is, that you should throw your thoughts on paper with the same ease with which they fall from your lips. When you sit down to write a letter, imagine that you are sitting down to talk to a friend ; and if you adopt a style of elegant conversation, you will adopt the very best style for a correspondence.

You will not understand me as prescribing any exact

order for your studies, when I mention, next, arithmetic. I hardly need say that this is important, not so much, in the common acceptation of the word, as an accomplishment, as it is for the every-day, practical purposes of life ; so that there is hardly a condition in which you can suppose yourself placed, but that your ignorance of this branch must, at some time or other, subject you not only to sad mortification, but to sore inconvenience. Of the new mode of calculating, commonly called mental arithmetic, I am unable to speak from much practical knowledge ; but I must confess that the results of this mode of teaching which I have witnessed, even in small children, have surprised me ; and I have no doubt that it is the most easy and successful mode of communicating this kind of knowledge which has yet been discovered. But leaving to your instructors to decide in respect to the best manner of your studying arithmetic, I must insist that you make thorough work of it; insomuch that no calculation which you will have occasion to make, will ever embarrass you.

As to the higher branches of mathematics, if you have even a common relish for them, I think you may pursue them to some extent with advantage. If you are passionately fond of them, I would say unhesitatingly, better prosecute them so far as inclination may dictate and opportunity admit. But if your taste points you decidedly to a different course of study, and you find nothing in this branch to attract or interest you, why, then I would consent that your mathematical studies should be arrested at almost any point you please, after you have become thoroughly acquainted with common arithmetic. Algebra and geometry, however, it were certainly desirable should come into your course; and if you have intelligently advanced thus far, it is more than probable that your inclination will lead you still further. It is scarcely possible that you will ever be placed in circumstances in which these higher branches will come into direct use; nevertheless you may advantageously study them simply as a matter of intellectual discipline. It is an admirable way of learning to think on general subjects with precision, and to reason with clearness and force.

Of geography, I surely need not say any thing to you in the way of urging its importance or recommending it to your attention. When studied intelligently and with the proper helps, it possesses attractions to most minds which are irresistible. And to say nothing of the interest which belongs to it in itself considered, it is, as I think Lord Chesterfield remarks, one of the eyes of history. You will make yourself familiar with the earth, not only as it is known to the moderns, but as it was known to the ancients, as a preparation for the study both of ancient and modern history. It were scarcely necessary to add, that your acquisitions in this department of knowledge must be made principally from the map or the globe, as all impressions which you derive in any other way will be comparatively feeble and evanescent. The construction of maps also you will find a pleasant exercise, while it will serve to render your geographical knowledge more distinct and abiding.

I have adverted to history. This I would have you study not merely with a view to gratify curiosity, but as containing an instructive record of human actions, and as furnishing an important means of becoming acquainted with the operations of the human heart; for what the nature of man has been, so it is now; and its operations are the same, making due allowance for diversity of circumstances. In your attention to this branch, I would advise you first to make yourself thoroughly acquainted with some judicious outline of history; and so far as possible to fill up every part of the outline by your subsequent reading. In no branch of study will you need the aid of system more than this; and though you may accumulate materials without end, yet if you fail to reduce them to order, so that they shall be in your mind as so many distinct and well-arranged classes of facts, you will be able to use them to little advantage. While I would have you familiar with every part of history, both ancient and modern, I would recommend a special attention to the history of your own country; not only because it is your own, but because it is the land which seems to be marching forward in the order of Providence to a more glorious destiny than any other. Every thing seems to indicate that this country is to have a most important part in the final renovation of the world, and this surely is a reason why those who have their lot cast in it should understand well its history, that they may contemplate the wonderful works of God by which it has already been distinguished, and in which no doubt will be found the elements of its ultimate destiny.

Next to history, perhaps, may properly come mental and moral philosophy. These are indeed distinct branches, but as they both relate to the essential constitution of man, they may properly enough be noticed together. If you will prosecute them with success, you must bring to your aid much patient reflection; for you may rest assured that any superficial attention to these branches will be to no purpose. Every principle laid down in your text-book you must test by a reference to your own intellectual or moral constitution; and if you find a disagreement between the principle as it is stated by your author, and as it exists in your own bosom, you have reason to inquire whether your author be not in the wrong; for the original principles of human nature, and the operation of these principles, are substantially the same in persons of every class. The study of these branches, conducted in this way, you will readily perceive, is only the study of human character and human duty; and surely this cannot be unworthy to employ your faculties, whether as an intellectual being, or as a probationer for eternity.

Some degree of attention you may properly bestow upon mechanical philosophy and chemistry. These, together with kindred sciences which come under the general department of natural history, while they answer important practical purposes, are admirably adapted to enlarge our views of the wisdom and power and goodness of the Creator. If your circumstances should permit, and your taste should incline you to bestow some attention upon several of the branches of natural science, I should not object to it ; but if you should confine yourself to one or two, mechanical philosophy and chemistry would probably best reward your efforts.

As to modern languages, I am not particularly desirous that you should aim at very high attainments. Of the French I should be glad to have you acquire so much knowledge that you can read it with fluency and correctness ; but as for Spanish, Italian, and other modern languages, there is so little in them which it were worth your while to read, that you have my full consent for never opening a grammar of either. The dead languages I do not regard as constituting an important part of female education ; and yet, if your taste should incline you to it, I confess I should be gratified to see you able to converse with the mighty dead of Grecian and Roman fame, and still more to see you able to read the Scriptures in the languages in which they were dictated by the Holy Ghost. This last I know is a rare acquisition for a young lady, but it is one which, in my eye at least, always serves to elevate her character.

I cannot conclude this list of studies without recommending to you a careful attention to the evidences of Christianity ; and I rejoice to find that in some of our female seminaries, this is already recognized as a distinct branch of education. Every part of this subject is full of interest, but no part of it, perhaps, grows upon the mind so much, on reflection, as that which relates immediately to the word itself—what is popularly termed the internal evidence. Nearly identified with the study of this, is the study of the doctrines of the gospel ; and I earnestly hope the time is not far distant when a knowledge of some outline of scripture truth, or what perhaps is still better, the Bible itself, will be considered essential to a complete female education.

You perceive I have said nothing of merely ornamental branches. The reason is, not that I regard them as absolutely unimportant, but only comparatively so. I am willing, if your circumstances admit, that you should attend to drawing, painting, or music, or all of them, provided only you have a natural taste for them, and do not suffer them to interfere with your improvement in more important branches. I say, *if you have a taste for them*, for nothing seems to me more ridiculous than for a girl utterly destitute of taste to spend months in trying to learn the use of the pencil, while neither she nor her friends are to reap any other reward of her labors, than is found in the awkward result of having a few pictures to amuse, or as the case may be, to frighten her younger sisters. If you have a talent for music, I am more than willing that you should cultivate it; for it will not only supply you with innocent, and I may say, elegant amusement, but it may often banish mel ancholy from your mind, and refresh and invigorate the spirits of your friends. But I repeat, let every accomplishment of this kind be suffered to hold only its proper place. If you find that your attention to these or any kindred branches is at any time making you indifferent to the more solid parts of your educa- tion, especially if you find that it serves to cherish in you a spirit of vanity, and to diminish your interest in the realities of religion, you need no better evidence that it has become excessive; and that however inno- cent these things may be in themselves, there is danger that you will pervert them to your injury or ruin.

I am your devoted

FATHER.

LETTER V.

EDUCATION—DOMESTIC ECONOMY.

My DEAR CHILD—However much you may be distinguished for intellectual cultivation, or for proficiency in the more refined and ornamental branches, you can make no claim to a complete education, unless you are well acquainted with domestic economy. I am aware that this is a subject which from some cause or other many young females regard with strong aversion; and there is reason to fear, that in too many instances this aversion is heightened by receiving in some degree the parental sanction; but you may rely on it, there cannot be a greater mistake on the subject of female education, than to suppose that this branch of it may with safety be neglected. With regard to the extent to which you should be informed on this subject, I would say in general, that you ought to have so much knowledge of it as will enable you to regulate with advantage the concerns of a family. There are indeed some of the domestic arts which you can hardly be expected to acquire; and which, in the ordinary walks of domestic life, may not be important; but whatever relates to the immediate superintendence and direction of household concerns, you cannot neglect without exposing yourself to inconvenience which no future exertions may be able completely to remedy.

It is important that you should cultivate a taste for the management of domestic concerns as early as possible. As no part of your education is more practical than this, it were unsafe to neglect it even for a short period, as the consequence of such neglect would probably be, that you would form other habits uncongenial with domestic employments, and which perhaps might give you an aversion to them which you would never overcome. Do not consider it a hardship, therefore, to be placed in circumstances which favor your attention to this subject, and even demand your active exertions. Every item of this kind of knowledge which you gain, you will be able hereafter to turn to some practical account, which will compensate many fold for the labor of attaining it.

It is not uncommon for young females in the higher walks of life, to satisfy themselves in the neglect of this branch of education on the ground that their lot is cast in circumstances of opulence and splendor. If this excuse could ever be sustained, you have no right to expect that your condition in life will allow you to avail yourself of it; but the truth is, that it cannot be admitted in *any* case. For what if Providence should actually place you in circumstances of wealth, and what the world calls independence? Would you not still be as truly accountable to God for all your possessions, as though you had been limited to a moderate competence? Nay, would not your responsibility be increased just in proportion to the abundance which had been bestowed upon you? This therefore, instead of being an argument for the neglect of the domestic part of your education, is actually a reason why you should attend to it with the greater care; for if a profusion of the bounties of heaven be intrusted to your management, and you are responsible for the proper improvement of them all, is it not preëminently desirable that you should possess that knowledge which will enable you to acquit yourself as a faithful steward?

But if you leave the idea of accountableness entirely out of the question, there are still other reasons of great weight why this part of your education should not be neglected. Without a proper attention to it, you can never be qualified to preside in the concerns of a family. Though you should be placed in a station which might enable you to command all the conveniences and assistance which opulence can furnish, you will never feel at home in your own house, unless you have yourself that practical knowledge which will enable you to keep your house in order. You cannot realize half the value of your domestic aid, unless you are capable of exercising a general superintendence, and giving proper directions; and without such ability,

you will be liable to constant impositions from those
to whom you will be obliged to confide interests which
ought to remain exclusively in your own hands. Many
a large estate has been squandered, and many a family
reduced to want, in consequence of a deficiency in this
part of female education.

Let me add, if Providence should ever place you at
the head of a family, and you are obliged, from ignorance of domestic economy, to intrust its concerns to
another, you cannot maintain the dignity which appropriately belongs to such a station. You will be subject to a thousand painful mortifications from discover-
ing that your concerns are improperly managed, and
yet being unable to suggest the proper remedy; and
though you may try to flatter yourself that your
ignorance on this subject may pass for evidence of
a genteel education, it is more than probable that
the unsavory food which will sometimes chance to be
placed before your guests, will lead them to regret
that you happened to possess so unfortunate an accomplishment.

What I have said hitherto on this subject has been
principally upon the supposition that you are to be
placed in circumstances of external ease and affluence.
But I hardly need say that this is by no means certain.
Even if your prospects in this respect should be fair at
the commencement of domestic life, there are a thousand changes which may await you, any one of which
may cast around you the gloom and desolation of

heart-breaking poverty. I could tell you of many who
have begun life without a cloud being seen to settle
upon their temporal prospects, and have closed it in
all the degradation and wretchedness which the most
abject want could occasion. I would fondly indulge
the hope that Heaven may avert such a lot as this
from my dear child; but as it is impossible to tell
what scenes of adversity the changes of life may bring
with them, it is unquestionably the part of wisdom
that you should be prepared for any lot to which
Providence may call you. What then, if you should
be destined in a few years to the obscure and humble
walks of poverty? What if from the comfortable
competence you now possess, you should sink to a
condition upon which you have hitherto been scarcely
able to look, without feelings of compassion and tears
of sympathy? What if you should see around you a
little defenceless family, and all the dreaded evils of
poverty clustering upon them in melancholy profusion?
And what if, in the midst of all these circumstances
of external depression, you should be found incapable
of devising a plan or lifting a hand for the relief or
comfort of yourself and family? In supposing this
case, believe me, I am not dealing in fiction: I have
seen an elegant, accomplished female, brought up in
the lap of luxury, in these very circumstances : and
who knows but that another such case may occur, and
that it may not be the case of my beloved child?
Sure I am that another argument cannot be necessary

to impress you with the importance ot the subject I
am endeavoring to urge.

And now, if I have gained your conviction to the
importance of this branch of education, let me repeat
the request that you will begin without delay to make
it a practical matter.   I know indeed, that much de-
pends in this case on maternal attention and effort;
but I know too, that there is in some young females
an aversion to domestic employments, which a mother's
persevering exertions do not overcome; and I also
know that little improvement can reasonably be expected in any department of knowledge, in which the
mind does not act not only without constraint, but with
alacrity.   And I beg you to bear in mind, that the
knowledge of which I am speaking is to be acquired
only in a single way, and that is by actual experience.
You may study the science of domestic economy as
carefully as you will, and you may receive lessons
from experienced and skilful managers, and after all,
you will be little wiser till you come down to the
actual reality of participating in the every-day concerns of a family.   When you actually put your hand
to the work, you will begin to learn; but unless you
put your hand to it frequently, and learn to think it
no dishonor to engage in any thing appertaining to
the economy of a family, you can never expect to become an accomplished housekeeper.   In a preceding
letter I have urged upon you the importance of taking
a good degree of exercise; let me here say, that you

cannot comply with that direction to better purpose
than by spending a part of every day in domestic employments.   And while it will secure to you the benefit
of relaxation from your studies, and of the exercise of
your bodily powers, it will be an effectual—the only
effectual means of preparing you to appear with honor
and usefulness in this department, as the head of a
family.

In connection with this general subject, I have a
word to say in respect to the regulation of your expenses.   In all your dealings I would have you avoid
even the appearance of being parsimonious; let no one
ever have just occasion to say, in respect to any pecuniary transaction of yours, that it has not been perfectly liberal and honorable.   Nevertheless there is an
ostentation of liberality which I would have you carefully avoid; for it is really a contemptible quality, and
so the world regard it.   There is also in some young
females a spirit of extravagance—a disposition to incur expenses which their condition in life neither demands nor justifies; another quality which deserves
severe reprobation.   I trust I shall never be subjected
to the mortification of seeing exemplified in you either
of these dispositions.   Let your expenditures be regulated, not merely by a regard to your ability, but to
your accountableness as a steward of the divine bounty.
Regard economy as a virtue, and never be unwilling
to be seen in the practice of it.   It is a shame to any
steward to waste his Lord's goods.   It is honorable

to contract your personal expenses as far as you may, that you may thereby have the more ability to succor the needy and distressed.

I will close this letter by suggesting a hint or two on the subject of dress; as it is in relation to this, more perhaps than any thing else, that most young females are tempted to indulge in extravagance. I would always have you appear in this respect neat and decent, and do not care how much correct taste you display; but I beg you to avoid all gaudy and superfluous ornament. It is a good rule to follow the fashion in dress just so far that you shall not be marked as singular. But you may rely on it, that a disposition to take the lead in fashions, to shine forth in splendid apparel, and even to profane the house of God by a gaudy glare of lace and gold, is always taken with discerning people as proof of a weak head or a proud heart. In the circle of my acquaintance there is a family of young ladies who have a fortune which few females in this country have ever inherited. They have been educated in a style of princely liberality; and I may say, with the voice of all their acquaintances to sustain me, that they are the ornament of their sex. These young ladies have their hearts and hands open to every object of charity within their reach; but in their dress there are scarcely any females in the surrounding population who are equally simple and unpretending. And who, think you, regards them the less for this trait in their character?

Believe me, every one regards them the more. There is in it a charming simplicity, a right estimate of things, which attracts universal admiration. I would say to every young female, I would especially say to you, "Go and do likewise."

Your devoted

FATHER.

LETTER VI.

GENERAL READING.

MY DEAR CHILD—In the course of your education, and after it is completed, you will occasionally find leisure to devote to miscellaneous reading. As this is one of the principal means by which you will become acquainted with the sentiments of others, you will readily perceive that it cannot but exert, either for good or evil, an important influence on your character. It is the design of this letter to furnish you some hints which may assist you to regulate this employment, so that it shall be at once the most useful and the most agreeable.

And the first suggestion which I would offer on this subject is, that all your reading should be, as far as possible, with some definite object other than merely to occupy your time. If you have no object in view, you may be sure that you will accomplish none ; and thus your reading will be at best a mere waste of time, and not improbably will be fraught with positive intellectual or moral evil. When you take up a book, decide if you can, from its title, or its table of contents, what good purpose you can accomplish by reading it, what faculties of your mind it will be likely to improve, or what moral dispositions to refine or elevate; and having settled this point, if the book be worthy of your attention, you can hardly fail to be benefited by reading it.

Another remark closely connected with the preceding is, that you should never allow yourself to read without reflection. There is no habit more easily acquired than that of occupying the eye merely upon an author, and leaving the mind to its own wanderings; and there is scarcely any habit which, in the end, more completely unstrings the intellect, and renders it incapable of commanding its own powers. The legitimate design of reading is, not to supersede, but to assist reflection—not to put the faculties to sleep, but to brighten them by active exercise. Different books, it is acknowledged, require different degrees of mental exertion; but you may take it for granted, that a book which is not worth the labor of some thought, is not worth the labor of reading. Whatever book you may have in hand, let your mind be just as intensely employed as is necessary to enable you to realize the full advantage of reading it; that is, to enable you to comprehend its full meaning, and to give it, so far as may be desirable or practicable, a lodgment in your memory. If you find your thoughts at any time wandering obstinately from your author, and if no effort will bring them under your control, so that you can read to advantage, and such cases will sometimes occur from mere physical derangement, better lay aside your book than to continue reading in this attitude of mental vacancy. You will be none the wiser for what you read, and you may be forming an intellectual habit which will diminish your power of acquiring wisdom in more favored circumstances.

It follows, from the remark just made, that you should be on your guard against reading too much. There is such a thing as a diseased intellectual appetite, which craves an excess of food, and is only satisfied with devouring every thing that comes in its way. But to indulge such an appetite were just as preposterous as to think of nourishing the body by taking a quantity of food which should altogether exceed the digestive powers of the system. If you would read to advantage, you must incorporate what you read with your own thoughts, and gather from it materials for future reflection. But this you can never do, if your whole time is occupied in reading, or if you take up one volume after another in such rapid succession that your mind can retain no distinct impression of the contents of any of them. Some of the minds which have shone most brilliantly, have been but little occupied with books, being far more conversant with their own thoughts than the thoughts of others. Remember that a few books carefully read, and thoroughly di-

gested, and used as helps to intellectual exertion, will
be of far more use to you than scores of volumes
which are gone through with little thought, and the
contents of which either instantly pass out of the mind,
or remain in it an indigested mass of materials.

But while you should avoid reading too much, it is
desirable, that of the books which, you *do* read, you
should form a habit of selecting and treasuring up
those parts which are most important. You cannot
expect to retain the whole of any book; and if you
should attempt it, you would probably lose the whole
by tasking your memory so severely; but even if it
were possible, it would ordinarily be to no good purpose, as there is much in almost every book, which
might be in your mind without at all increasing your
stock of useful knowledge. That you may possess
yourself of the substance of what you read, make it a
point to review your author before you lay him aside,
and form an analysis, at least in your own mind, of all
that you have been reading. It will be well too, if
you commit to paper a general outline of every important book you read; or at least, that you make
references on a blank page, to those parts to which
you may afterwards wish to recur. Some such expe-
dient as this will be of great use in assisting your
recollection, and will help you to retain stores of
knowledge which would otherwise be inevitably lost
from your memory.

You will, moreover, find great advantage in having

the different departments of literature and science with which you are conversant, so far systematized in your mind that you will be able to refer every book that you read to some one of them. In this way, your mind will become an intellectual storehouse, accommodated to the reception of every kind of useful materials; and its various apartments arranged with so much skill and order, that you will never be at a loss where to deposit any new article of knowledge, or where to find any you had previously deposited. On the other hand, if you read without any regard to order, as it respects your previous acquisitions, the impressions which are made upon your mind will be vague and indistinct; and after a little while the severest effort will be ineffectual to recall them.

Having thrown out these few hints in respect to the manner of your reading, suffer me now to add some brief suggestions in respect to the selection of books.

And first of all, let me say to you, never allow yourself, from any consideration, to read books of immoral tendency. A bad book, like a bad friend, may exert an influence which an established habit of virtue will scarcely be able to resist; and where a corrupt association is once formed in the mind, it is exceedingly difficult to destroy it: it remains there, a leprous spot, usually bidding defiance to every thing but the power of divine grace. What though a book of this character may fall into your hands, which is rendered peculiarly attractive by a refined and fasci-

nating style? You are to bear in mind, that these
literary embellishments can no more disarm false
principles of their fatal tendency, than poison can
lose its virulence by being mingled with honey. Nay,
these very attractions give to bad books much of their
dangerous influence; for while they recommend them
to the attention of the incautious and inexperienced,
they too often serve as a channel through which the
most deadly impressions are conveyed to the mind.
And if the reading of such books were the only way
in which you could gain the refinement of literature,
then I would say, better remain in ignorance for ever
than hazard the wreck of your moral principles, or
admit into your heart the elements of destruction.

But while you carefully avoid all works which are
fitted in any degree to corrupt the principles or sully
the purity of the mind, I would have you select those
which, on the whole, are best adapted to increase your
stock of useful knowledge and practical wisdom. In
the wide range of elegant literature, there is a great
variety of authors which will at once enlighten your
understanding, improve your taste, and exert an influence upon your heart favorable to virtue and piety.
The entire works of Mrs. More, the pride and glory of
your sex, you cannot read too often or too attentively.
They contain a system of moral instruction, particularly adapted to young females, which has perhaps
never had a parallel in any age or country.

It is an error, against which you should be on your

guard in the selection of your reading, to confine yourself exclusively to books of a particular kind. The
effect of this would be to corrupt your taste, to destroy
the proportion which exists among the various powers
of your mind, and, as the case may be, to expose you
to serious inconvenience and mortification. That you
may avoid this evil, endeavor to be conversant with
those authors who have been most conspicuous in the
various departments of literature. Such a course will
be likely to give you a correct and dignified taste, at
the same time that it will impart a general consistency
and vigor to your intellectual character.

Though I have no wish that you should be an en-
thusiast with regard to poetry, I would still have you
in some degree familiar with the best poets both of
ancient and modern date. The immortal works of
Milton, Cowper, and Thompson, may be read with
great advantage to the heart as well as the understanding. But there are others, usually associated in
the same cluster of poetical genius, who, however exquisite their poetry, cannot be safely recommended as
guides to youthful virtue. Much of the modern poetry,
I am sorry to say, is chargeable with the same immoral
tendency. Byron, with a genius to which few, whether
of ancient or modern days, can lay claim, has clouded
his brilliant and beautiful conceptions with the dark
hue of infidelity and moral death; and so long as his
writings last, they must stand as a monument of a
noble intellect prostituted to the worst of all purposes,

that of corrupting and destroying his fellow-men.
Moore, with less of genius than Byron, has written, for
the most part, for no better purpose ; and it were far
worse than a waste of time to employ yourself upon
his productions.   Even the poetry of Sir Walter Scott,
though it has much in it to delight the imagination, is
greatly deficient in moral sentiment, and seems scarcely
fitted for any higher purpose than to furnish a light
kind of amusement.   James Montgomery belongs to
an entirely different class, or rather, he stands nearly
alone ; and I have no hesitation in assigning to him a
preëminence among the poets of the present day.
With an invention uncommonly fertile in whatever is
chaste and beautiful, he unites a deep and strong religious sensibility ; and in reading his poetry, you see
not less of the Christian than of the poet : you feel
that your imagination and all your powers are in
communion with an exalted genius, while you seem to
breathe a pure and moral atmosphere, and to have
your soul attracted towards a region of perfect purity.
I might mention also the lamented Pollok, who lived
long enough to show that God had given him noble
powers, and that he was disposed to employ them in
his Master's service ; who wrote but little, but in that
little has erected for himself a bright and enduring
monument.   So too I might speak of Mrs. Hemans,
whose poetry is the subject of much and deserved
praise ; and of many others, of various degrees of
merit, all of whom are unexceptionable in their moral

tendency. But it is unnecessary that I should enlarge on this subject, as I have no doubt that, with the hints already given, I may safely leave it to your own taste and judgment.

As for dramatic writers, I cannot say that I am desirous that you should cultivate a taste for them. The plays of Shakespeare are incomparably the finest specimen of dramatic genius which the English language preserves; and it cannot be denied that they exhibit human life and manners with great power and beauty and effect; but it is equally unquestionable that there is much in them to call into exercise the worst passions of human nature, to tarnish the purity of the mind, and to beget a kind of profane familiarity with things of high and sacred import. I should expect, therefore, that the loss you would sustain from reading them, in point of moral feeling, would be greater than any advantage you would gain in respect to intellectual improvement. And on no account could I consent to your reading them, unless it were under the direction of some judicious friend, who would select for you the parts which are most unexceptionable. Addison, Young, and a few others have written plays which may perhaps be considered unexceptionable; but I must confess, I should feel no regret if you should think it best to dispense with this class of authors altogether.

But there is no species of reading to which young females are usually more inclined than that of novels,

or from which they are so much in danger. I will
not say that there are no works of this kind which indicate a tone of correct moral feeling, and which are of
unexceptionable moral tendency. Nor will I take it
upon me to pass severe judgment upon many persons
of great excellence who have indulged in this kind of
reading, on the ground that it furnishes many important lessons in respect to the operations of the human
heart. But I must say, after an attentive consideration of this subject, and withal, after having once held
a somewhat different opinion, that I do not wish you
ever to read a novel. For, admit that the novels of
Richardson, and some of the modern novels of Scott,
and a few others, abound with critical views of human
nature, and contain many specimens of eloquent writing, and in their direct moral influence may be regarded as harmless, I cannot doubt that the time
which you would occupy in reading them might be
employed to better purpose in studying the actual
realities of life, as they are exhibited by the biographer
or the historian ; and moreover, there is danger, if you
begin to read works of fiction, with an intention to
read but few, and to confine yourself to the better
class, that your relish for these productions will increase, till you can scarcely feel at home unless the
pages of a novel are spread out before you ; and what
is still more to be dreaded, that you will read indiscriminately the most corrupt as well as the least exceptionable. You may rest assured that a character

formed under the influence of novel reading, is miserably fitted for any of the purposes of practical life. The imagination being hereby wrought into a feverish state, gains the ascendency over the judgment, and a thousand bright visions rise up before the mind, which experience proves to be unreal. This species of reading, moreover, inspires a disgust for the sober and practical realities in which we have to mingle; and what is worse than all, it often closes every avenue through which the awful truths of religion can be conveyed to the heart. I say then, as you would avoid forming a character which combines all the elements of insipidity, corruption, and moral death, beware of the reading of novels. Many a young female has been obliged to trace to this cause the destruction of her principles, her character, and ultimately her life; and if she have escaped these greater evils, she is still unfitted for solid intellectual enjoyment, and for a life of active usefulness.

I would have you bestow considerable·attention on the periodical publications of the day, though you ought here, as much as in any department of literature, to read with discrimination. Of these publications you need not to be told that there is every variety, from the dignified quarterly, that exercises an almost unlimited sway in the region of taste and letters, down to the contemptible catchpenny paper, that lives by circulating slander and falsehood. It would be well, if your circumstances should permit, that you should accustom yourself regularly to read one of the great foreign reviews; and of those in our own country, which are purely or chiefly literary, you may advantageously select one or two more. But in reading these publications, even the best of them, you ought not tamely to surrender your own judgment of an author to the dictation of these literary censors; but to let their opinion pass for only what it is worth; and if it have been formed under the influence of partiality, or prejudice, to let it pass for nothing. Of religious periodicals it may be well for you to select one from each of the most important classes; as, for instance, one that is devoted to theological review and discussion, one to missionary intelligence, etc. By selecting your reading of this kind with care, and keeping yourself within certain limits, you will gain far more information, and with much less labor, than if you were to devour, indiscriminately, every periodical that should fall in your way.

You will find it a useful employment occasionally to read judicious books of travels. It happens, unfortunately, that most works of this kind seem to have been written with too little regard to truth; and instead of having the sober results of actual experience, we have had the wild and wonderful, and sometimes ridiculous sallies of the writer's imagination. There is probably no species of writing, in respect to which you ought to make more abatement from glaring and marvellous statements than this, not only because authors of this kind, from their rapid observations, are often liable to mistake, but because certainty has such an advantage over conjecture, that they are under a strong temptation not only to speak, but to speak positively, where it would be honest for them to confess that they know nothing. We are perfectly aware how much the character of our own country has been traduced and held up to ridicule by travellers from abroad ; and it is fair to conclude that much that professes to be the record of travels in other countries is equally at war with truth and justice. Some of the best books of foreign travels have been written by missionaries, from this country and England ; and I doubt not that it is from this source that we are hereafter to gain our most accurate knowledge of the population, the manners, and general statistics of other countries.

Biography is a species of reading which is fitted to amuse, while it instructs you. It brings out before you the human character, and often in circumstances of the deepest interest ; and holds up a mirror in which you may see the operations of your own heart. I regret to say that well executed and attractive works of this kind, are far less common in the English language than could be desired. Among the most interesting within my knowledge are the biographies of Philip and Matthew Henry, the latter of which was written, and the former revised, by my excellent and highly valued friend, Doctor Williams of Shrewsbury.

Within a few years many highly interesting works
have been published, commemorating the character
and services of distinguished missionaries, and those
who have been especially active in the missionary
cause, such as Martin, Richmond, Burder,. Rowland
Hill, etc. I would advise you, especially, to become
familiar with the characters who have been most
conspicuous in our own country, and who have been
instrumental of transmitting to us our goodly inheritance. You may also study with great advantage the
lives of many distinguished females of modern times,
such as Mrs. Graham, Mrs. Huntington, Mrs. Newell,
and others who have gone to heaven, leaving a bright
track of glory behind them. Whenever you engage
in this kind of reading, endeavor to turn it to some
account in the improvement of your heart. Whatever
excellence you discover in the character you are contemplating, endeavor to make it your own; whatever
error, fortify yourself against it with renewed vigilance; whatever weakness, see whether it be not the
besetting infirmity of your own nature; whatever victory over temptation, whatever serenity amidst sorrow,
whatever triumph in death, let it lift your eye and
your heart upwards, for that almighty grace by which
those blessings are secured. The reading of biography
in this way I must most cordially recommend, as it
cannot fail to make you wiser and better.

You will anticipate me when I say that I wish you
to be conversant with the best works on theology.

In many of the old writers of the seventeenth century, which are now little read, at least by females, you will find treasures of thought and devotion, which would amply reward you for the labor of examining them. Owen, Baxter, Flavel, Charnock, Bates, and Howe, though they possess indeed different degrees of merit, yet are all rich in evangelical sentiment, and some of them distinguished by a bold and powerful eloquence. The entire works of any of these authors are voluminous, and perhaps not easily accessible; but some of the most popular and useful treatises of each of them, and of many others of the same school, are within your reach, and may be read without occupying an undue portion of your time. If I should mention any one as deserving a preference above the rest, I think it would be Howe. There is running through his writings a majesty of conception, and a deep current of devotional feeling, which I look for in vain, in the same degree, in almost any other writer.

I wish you to read attentively at least one system of theology. Mere miscellaneous reading on theological subjects, however useful it may be, can never give you a distinct and connected view of the great system of revealed truth. There is no work within my knowledge, so well adapted to answer this purpose, as the admirable system of theology by the late President Dwight. It may look a little formidable to you at first, but I am almost sure that if you once engage in reading it, you will not be impatient to find its close.

While the subjects are arranged with philosopnical accuracy, they are discussed with a degree of perspicuity, force, and eloquence, for which I think you will look in vain in any similar work. There are other books containing systems of theology which you might read with advantage, but instead of recommending any of them to your particular attention, I would advise you, when you have gone through with Doctor Dwight once, to begin and go through with him again. This course I would recommend, not from a desire to disparage other authors, but from a conviction that to read and digest this as you ought, would be of more use to you than to read several similar works superficially; and withal, that you could expect to find little in other bodies of divinity that would be of much importance, which this does not contain.

You will also occasionally employ yourself in reading sermons. As your first object here should be the improvement of your heart, you should select those which are distinguished by an earnest and practical exhibition of divine truth. But it is perfectly consistent that you should combine, with the culture of your affections, the improvement of your mind; and for this purpose, you should choose those which are composed with the best taste, and with the greatest degree of intellectual vigor. The sermons of Barrow and Jeremy Taylor, though they partake much of the spirit of the age in which they were written, are specimens of a vigorous and powerful eloquence, to which modern times have hardly furnished a parallel. The sermons of Archbishop Tillotson are fertile in weighty and impressive sentiment, and on subjects connected with natural religion are exceeded by few in the language. Bishop Sherlock's sermons, though in some minor points not exactly accordant with my own views of religious truth, are certainly a monument of an elegant and active mind, which posterity can never cease to admire. The sermons of the immortal Edwards, though wholly destitute of ornament, are in the highest degree instructive, and contain perhaps the most powerful appeals to the heart and conscience which are to be found out of the Bible. President Davies' sermons have justly acquired a high celebrity for a dignified, forcible, and solemn exhibition of divine truth, and for a devotional fervor and sacred unction, which indicate that they were dictated by a heart full of faith and of the Holy Ghost. The sermons of Robert Walker, a modern Scotch divine, are fine specimens of an evangelical spirit, and admirably adapted to promote the influence of practical religion. Jay's sermons are full of truth and life and beauty, and are fitted to be alike gratifying to a refined taste, and an elevated piety. The sermons of the late Doctor Lathrop are written with great simplicity, and discover a fertility of invention, a grasp of intellect, an enlightened view of scripture doctrine, and an elevation of pious feeling, which, to say the least, are not often found in combination. Doctor Mason's sermons are

distinguished for bold and elevated thought, for a style
of classical elegance, and for overwhelming appeals to
the understanding and the heart.   The sermons of Dr.
Chalmers can hardly fail to be read with interest, as
the offspring of an inventive and powerful mind, and
as containing a lucid exhibition of divine truth ; though
it were much to be desired that the style in which
they are written had been less diffuse and involved.
Robert Hall is, in my opinion, the first writer of sermons of the age.   The irresistible force of his reasoning, the beauty and grandeur of his thoughts, and the
dignified and graceful manner in which they are expressed, in connection with the truly evangelical spirit
which pervades them, render his sermons as perfect
specimens of this kind of writing, perhaps, as the world
may expect to see.   I might extend this list almost
indefinitely, but I am willing to leave much to your
own judgment ; and those which have been mentioned
are probably enough to occupy as much leisure as you
will be able to give to this kind of reading.

Some portion of your religious reading will of course
be of a miscellaneous character.   Without attempting
to give you a list of books in this department, for I
should not know where to begin or where to end, I
will simply mention two or three authors whose works
appear to me to have a special claim upon your attention.   Wilberforce's Practical View has probably been
one of the most useful books which the present age
has produced.   Its influence in elevating the standard

of piety, especially in the higher circles in Great Britain, it is impossible adequately to estimate, and happily its circulation has been extended through almost every part of Protestant Christendom. In an interview which I was once privileged to hold with that venerable man, I remember his adverting with the highest gratification, and yet with the deepest humility, to the success with which God had been pleased to crown that effort of his for the advancement of evangelical truth and piety; and there was every thing in his remarks and in his manner of making them, to indicate that he regarded himself only as an unworthy instrument, and ascribed to God all the glory. The works of Doctor Dick of Scotland, in several volumes, beginning with "the Christian Philosopher," are exceedingly well worthy not only of being read, but diligently studied. No other writer within my knowledge has so happily illustrated the mutual relations of science and religion; and whoever can read his admirable works without finding the powers of his intellect quickened, and his reverence for the divine character increased, and his views of his own insignificance and unworthiness deepened, and a spirit of benevolence glowing more intensely in his bosom, must either be destitute of an understanding to comprehend what he reads, or must have a heart that is proof against the most hallowed, the most impressive exhibitions of divine truth. The writings of the Rev. John Angell James, consisting of several practical treatises on different subjects, as they have acquired a great and deserved popularity in this coun-try, will not, I trust, escape your attention. They are characterized by an uncommonly attractive style and copiousness and originality of thought, and exhibit the truths and duties of Christianity with great unction and loveliness. I perceive that a new work from this interesting writer is just announced, designed particu-larly to aid the inquiring sinner, and I have no doubt that it will prove a most useful auxiliary to the cause of revivals.

I cannot conclude this letter without urging you to a diligent and daily perusal of the holy Scriptures. Remember that this is the great fountain of wisdom ; that it contains an infallible record of the dispensations of God towards our world ; that it faithfully exhibits the character of man, and opens up a way by which he may attain to a glorious destination. Recollect, too, that there is nothing which approaches the Bible, as a mere human composition, in point of interest ; no other historical record of equal antiquity ; no other specimens with which those of the Scriptures can be compared, of beautiful simplicity or overpowering grandeur. You may find various important helps to the study of the Scriptures ; but there is none within my knowledge which I deem so important as the Intro-duction to the Study of the Scriptures, by the Rev. Thomas Hartwell Horne ; a work which for extent of well-digested biblical learning has scarcely a parallel

in the productions of any age.   I say again, then, read
the Bible attentively, every day of your life.   Read it
in its connection, observing carefully how one part of
it is illustrated and confirmed by another.   Read it
with a deep and practical impression that it contains
the words of eternal life—a message which he that
believeth shall be saved, and he that believeth not
shall be damned.   In this way your mind will become
early imbued with heavenly wisdom, your affections
will become purified and elevated, and your whole
character gradually conformed to that standard of
perfection which the Bible reveals.

With the earnest hope that you may obey these
directions, and thus become wise and good while you
are young,

I remain your ever affectionate

FATHER.

LETTER VII.

INDEPENDENCE OF MIND.

My dear Child—There is scarcely any quality which is more frequently the theme of eulogy among all classes, than that which is to constitute the subject of this letter. The good and the bad alike will extol something which each calls independence of mind; and all will agree, that the quality which is indicated by this language is an essential element in a truly noble character. But it is worthy of remark, that the expression has a variety of meaning with different individuals: that with some it indicates what is truly great and noble; with others, what is unlovely, and even odious: it becomes, therefore, a matter of importance that you should distinguish the precious from the vile—that you should take care to cultivate genuine independence of character, and not deceive yourself with something which has been unjustly complimented with the name.

Let me apprise you then, in the first place, that true independence is something entirely different from rashness. There are those who pride themselves on forming a hasty opinion, and adopting a course of conduct, even in relation to subjects of great moment, without stopping to look at the indications of Providence, or reflect at all on probable consequences. It matters little with them though they act entirely in the dark, provided only their movements are so rapid and boisterous as to excite attention. Persons of this character, you will always find, run themselves into a thousand needless difficulties. Even if they chance to go right, every judicious person will consider it a matter of mere accident, and to say the least, will give them far less credit for virtuous conduct, than if they had adopted the same course with forethought and deliberation.

True independence of the mind is equally unlike obstinacy, another quality with which it is often confounded. When a person has once formed an opinion and expressed it, especially with a great degree of confidence, and perhaps withal with some publicity, he is under strong temptation, from the pride of consistency, to retain that opinion, even in spite of light which ought to induce him to abandon it. The secret feeling of his heart is, that it would be a reflection either upon his discernment or his firmness, to avow a change in his convictions; and hence he endeavors to shut his eyes upon the evidence which might be likely to work such a change; or if the light is irresistible, and the change is forced upon him, he will refuse to acknowledge it, and will even act in a manner which he knows to be contrary to his own interest, rather than confess that he has been in a mistake. This is nothing short of the most pitiable obstinacy; and whoever exhibits it exposes himself to deserved contempt. Remember that it is an honor to confess an error as soon as you discover it, and as publicly as you may have avowed it. All will think the better of you for doing so; or if there be any exceptions, they are those whose praise is censure, and whose censure praise.

Equally remote is the quality which I would recommend from a contempt of the opinion of others. It is not uncommon to find persons who seem to regard their own opinion as infallible, and who treat the opinion of others with proportionate disrespect. No matter though the subject be one in respect to which they may be utterly ignorant, they will deliver their opinion with dictatorial confidence, and will treat every objection and every query as if it were, of course, the offspring of folly or impertinence. True independence, so far from giving its sanction to this spirit, disdains not to ask advice of the wise, and always treats their opinions with respect, though it does not yield to them an *implicit* consent. You need not fear that you will forfeit your character for decision, by asking judicious friends to counsel you on any important subject on which you may be called to act; indeed, a neglect to do so would justly expose you to the charge of vanity and presumption. On the subject of asking advice, however, let me give you two brief directions. One is, that you should consult only those whose advice is worthy of your attention ; the other is, that you should never consult any one after your decision is formed. It is nothing better than an insult to a friend, to go through the formality of asking his advice, and subjecting him to the trouble of giving it, when your opinion is decisively made up, and you only wish him to sanction it. You cannot adopt this course without some danger ; for if the individual whom you consult happens to discover the secret, he must be a good-natured person indeed not to be vexed at it : if he happens to advise you contrary to your predetermination, then you subject yourself to the unpleasant necessity of acting contrary to his opinion after you had formally sought it. It is wise to seek counsel of proper persons ; but it should always be to assist one to form an opinion, not merely to strengthen it after it is formed.

The independence which I wish you to cultivate is that quality which leads us to form all our opinions deliberately, and from the best light which we can gain, and then to adhere to them firmly and practically, until there shall be sufficient evidence to reverse our convictions.

This quality discovers itself in the very formation of opinions or principles. It keeps the mind steady amidst the conflicting views which may be presented before it. It causes it to look attentively at the evidence on every side, and to resist the undue influence of circumstances, and to form its conclusions after intelligent and impartial inquiry. Not that a person with this principle in operation will never be embarrassed with difficulties in respect to the path of duty : these difficulties may accumulate to such a degree, as to keep the mind for a long time in suspense ; but let them be formidable as they may, the mind will soberly and calmly consider them all, and will ultimately dispose of them to its own satisfaction. If you have genuine independence, then, it will keep you from inconsiderate and hasty judgments. It will save you from being enslaved to the opinions of others, and from adopting notions merely because they are current in the community around you. In short, it will subject you to the labor of forming your own judgments ; but when they are once formed it will insure to you the satisfaction of thinking that they are your own.

But this trait of character discovers itself, not only in the process by which we arrive at our convictions of what is true and right, but also in an intelligent adherence to those convictions after they are attained. It usually happens that those opinions which are formed most inconsiderately, are relinquished most easily ; whereas, they who have come to their conclusions by a process of deliberate and independent thought, rarely have occasion to change their views, and never, but upon the most patient and mature reflection. In other words, the mind that thinks for itself in the beginning, will almost of course continue to think for itself during the whole of its subsequent course. If difficulties arise in connection with any opinion which were not contemplated when that opinion was originally formed, they will of course be carefully weighed, and due importance will be given to them; but the mind will not be at the mercy of every caviller: unless there be new and decisive evidence of an opposite kind presented to it, in which case it would be obstinacy not to yield, it marches on in the strength and majesty of its own original convictions.

I have spoken of an independent mind as it discovers itself in forming and holding fast its own opinions. Let me add, that it is not less conspicuous in reducing principles to practice; in other words, in steadily persevering in what we believe to be duty. It requires far less strength of purpose to avow good principles, even in times of trial, than practically to exhibit those principles in an unyielding course of action. But as principles are nothing without practice, so it is the noblest office of genuine independence, to carry the mind forward in a course of action corresponding with its own convictions; to keep the hands nerved for effort when there may be a thousand pleas for relaxing exertion; and to give to this activity that direction only which conscience approves, when the strongest temptations offer themselves to an opposite course. You may dream of your own independence as much as you please, but unless it be of this practical kind which influences conduct as well as

opinions, and which is carried out into all the departments of human duty, you have much reason to believe
that neither you nor the world will be the better for
your having possessed it.

The advantages of an independent mind will readily
occur to you upon a moment's reflection.   One of them
is, that it furnishes the best security you can have, independently of a principle of Christian holiness, against
false principles and corrupt practice.   It is especially
in consequence of the want of this quality, that so
many young persons become victims to the most practical and fatal errors.   They are placed in circumstances in which it is fashionable to think lightly of
religion, or fashionable to disbelieve its truths; and
though at first conscience may remonstrate against
their throwing themselves into the current, yet they
have not strength of purpose to resist it; and principles which were at first adopted tremblingly, and with
severe compunction, are soon rendered more tolerable
by habit; and at no distant period they become the
governing principles of the life.   A proper share of
independence would keep you from adopting any opinions without due consideration; and if error in any of
its forms should be proposed to you, and you should
stop to canvass it, and should determine that you
would not receive it but upon deliberate and intelligent conviction, there is good reason to believe that
you would not receive it at all; for there is no fundamental error in religion or morals which is not seen to

be such by any one who examines it with due attention and impartiality.

It is another advantage of genuine independence, and ought to be with you a powerful motive for cultivating it, that it is fitted to give you a proper degree of self-respect. If you see an individual who betrays great indecision of character, and is a slave to the opinion of every body, having no opinion of his own, you cannot regard that individual other than with a species of pity, which borders well-nigh upon contempt. And the same must be true in respect to yourself: if you are conscious that you have no stability of purpose, and that your opinions of characters and things are not your own, but are taken upon trust, and that you do not think your own thoughts even upon the most common subjects, you may try to respect yourself, but you cannot; and moreover, you will be compelled to feel the mortifying conviction that others do not respect you. Whatever you or others may wish in regard to it, it is not in human nature that it should be otherwise. As you desire, therefore, to live in the favorable regards of others, or even of yourself, cultivate this trait which I am recommending.

And I may add, that this quality is not less essential to your usefulness. The fact that you had lost self-respect would destroy, in a great degree, your power of exertion; or, what is the same thing, would diminish the motives to it; and the fact that you had lost the respect of others would not only operate in the same

manner, but would tend to a similar result, by dimin-
ishing your opportunities of usefulness. And moreover, let your efforts be what they might, little real
good could be expected from them so long as they
were not subject to the direction of an independent
mind ; for if you should labor for a good object one
day, there could be no security that you would not
abandon it for an evil one the next ; or if you should
seem to be laboring successfully for a while, it is quite
probable that you might soon defeat your purpose by
some eccentric and ill-advised movement.   Under how
much greater advantages will your efforts be made if
you cultivate a suitable spirit of independence.   The
fact that you are conscious of doing right will render
your exertions easy and unembarrassed.   The. fact
that you have the respect and confidence of those
around you, will multiply your means of doing good.
And the fact that you are acting with reflection and
firmness, will impart an energy and efficiency to your
whole deportment.   As you would be spared the reproach of living to little or no purpose, let me say
again, cultivate a truly independent mind.

   As the most effectual means of making the attainment to which I have been urging you, let me counsel
you to cherish a deep sense of the constant presence
of God, and of your accountableness to him for every
part of your conduct.   An habitual impression of this
kind will make you comparatively indifferent, both to
the censures and applauses of mortals, and will lead

you to regard every other question as unimportant, in comparison with the simple question of duty. And the consequence of this cannot fail to be, that you will judge carefully and honestly of what is right, and will act with unyielding decision. No matter what temptations may spread themselves before you to divert you from the path of duty, the reflection, "Thou, God, seest me," brought home to your understanding and conscience, will insure you the victory over them. This is something distinct from natural inflexibility of character: it is independence of mind, based on religious principle; and it is this especially which I urge you to cultivate. That I may be permitted to see your character forming under the influence of this elevated principle, is the earnest wish of

Your affectionate

FATHER.

LETTER VIII.

FORMING THE MANNERS.

MY DEAR CHILD—Next in importance to the culture
of your heart and understanding, is the formation of
your manners.   You shall have the grounds on which
I form this opinion.

There are multitudes who will have no other crite-
rion than is hereby furnished, by which to judge of
your character.   In the varied intercourse of society,
you meet many persons, perhaps only for a single time
in the course of your life.   They almost of course form
some opinion of you ; and that opinion is built upon
what they witness of your general appearance.   With
good manners you may leave an impression upon a
stranger, from a casual meeting with him, which may
cause him to hold you in grateful remembrance through
life.   With manners of an opposite character you
would either be passed unnoticed, or perhaps remembered only as a glaring specimen of affectation or
rudeness.

It deserves also to be borne in mind, that in nearly
every case the first impressions of the character are

gathered from the manners; and every one knows that first impressions are not easily eradicated. Instances are not uncommon in which an individual, on the first introduction to another, has been struck with some apparent defect of disposition, as indicated by the manners; and though he may have been subsequently convinced that the impression was a mistaken one, has found it next to impossible·to forget it in the estimate he forms of the character. If your manners are as they should be, it will give you this great advantage in respect to every acquaintance you form— that the individual, from the beginning, will be prepossessed in your favor. If otherwise, the best you can hope is, that in finding your way ultimately into the favorable regards of other people, you will have to encounter a mass of prejudice.

But leaving first impressions out of view, there is something in the very constitution of human nature which inclines us to form a judgment of character from manners. It is always taken for granted, unless there is decisive evidence to the contrary, that the manners are the genuine expression of the feelings; and even where such evidence exists, that is, where we have every reason to believe that the external appearance does injustice to the moral dispositions, or, on the other hand, where the heart is too favorably represented by the manners, there is still a delusion practised upon the mind by what passes under the eye, which it is not easy to resist. You may take two

individuals of precisely the same degree of intellectual
and moral worth, and let the manners of the one be
bland and attractive, and those of the other distant
or awkward, and you will find that the former will
pass through life with far more ease and comfort
than the latter; for, though good manners will never
effectually conceal a bad heart, and are in no case
any atonement for it, yet, taken in connection with
amiable and virtuous dispositions, they naturally and
necessarily gain upon the respect and good-will of
mankind.

You will instantly perceive, if the preceding remarks
are correct, that it is not only your interest to cultivate
good manners, as you hereby recommend yourself to
the favorable regards of others, but also your duty, as
it increases, in no small degree, your means of usefulness. It will give you access to many persons, and
give you an influence over them, whom you could
otherwise never approach, much less whose feelings
and purposes you could ever hope in any measure to
control. I have known one instance at least, and I
doubt not that thousands of others have occurred, in
which an affectionate and winning manner has been
rendered instrumental, by the Holy Spirit, of breaking
up the delusions of impenitence; and, as I trust, of
saving a soul from death and hiding a multitude of
sins. In the very case to which I refer, I have little
doubt that an air of indifference or severity would have
closed up the avenues to the heart, and not improbably

barred it, in all future time, against the light and power of conviction.

There is yet another reason why this subject is deserving of your attention. It is, that as the manners derive their complexion in a great degree from the feelings, so the feelings are in turn influenced by the manners. Suppose, from your partiality to some friend, you should undertake to adopt some weak peculiarity in her deportment, it is more than probable, if the foolish experiment should succeed, that you would find yourself, at no distant period, with a set of feelings strongly assimilated to those of the individual whom you had sought to copy. Cultivate good manners, then, as one means of improving your dispositions, and imparting real excellence to your character.

That you may attain the object which I am recommending, let me advise you to lay the foundation aright, by cultivating good and amiable feelings. Without these, though you should attain what may pass with the world for good manners, they will only serve to convict you of hypocrisy; for, however it may be with others, you must yourself know that they do not indicate your real character. Endeavor then to banish from your heart all evil dispositions, and to cherish every temper that is amiable and praiseworthy. Resist, with unyielding firmness, the operations of pride, envy, jealousy, and every other bad passion. There are indeed infinitely higher motives which urge you to this course than are derived from its influence in forming your manners; though it is with reference to this exclusively that I direct your attention to it now. Nothing is so effectual a security for good manners, at least, nothing constitutes so good a foundation for them, as the spirit of Christianity. Let that reign in the heart, purifying, softening, elevating its various affections and propensities, and there you may look with confidence for an exhibition of genuine politeness.

In connection with the cultivation of benevolent feelings, it is necessary that you should acquire that habit of self-possession which will enable you at all times to act out your feelings without embarrassment. Where the manners are seen to indicate amiable moral qualities, and especially the gentle and benignant spirit of the gospel, this will go far to atone for any lesser imperfections by which they may be marked. Nevertheless, it is desirable that you should appear not only amiable, but unconstrained—that you should feel at ease yourself, and be able to put others at ease around you. You will be placed, almost of course, in a variety of situations: it is important that you should have that habitual self-command that will enable you readily to accommodate yourself to the peculiarities of each; and at least to conceal from those around you the secret that you are not perfectly at home. I do not say that this is essential to your passing in good society, but it certainly is essential to the perfection of good manners.

It is important also, that you should form a proper

estimate of your own relative standing in society, and
of what belongs to the various relations you sustain to
those around you. If you imagine yourself of more
consequence than you really are, it follows, almost of
course, that you will betray that opinion in an air of
self-respect which borders upon arrogance. If you
form too low an opinion of yourself, you will be likely
to make it manifest in a cringing manner, which cannot
fail to leave an impression of your inferiority. If you
form a true relative estimate of yourself, it will be a
security against the extremes both of arrogance and
of servility; it will render you dignified without being
haughty, condescending without sacrificing a proper
self-respect, and will make you acceptable alike in the
higher and lower walks of life.

I must not omit to mention that it is of great importance to the formation of good manners, that you
should be accustomed to mingle in good society. I do
not mean that you should select all your associates
from the more elevated walks of life, for this would
be likely to unfit you for mingling with ease and advantage among the lower classes; but I would have
you so much in cultivated society that you shall feel
perfectly at home, and that your manners shall appear
to have been formed upon a model of elegance and
refinement. It is a rare instance indeed, that a young
female who is habitually accustomed to society of a
rude or grovelling character, ever becomes graceful or
dignified in her own manners; and on the other hand,

where her intimate associates are persons of intelligence and refinement, it is almost a matter of course,
that she becomes conformed, in a good degree, to the
models with which she is conversant.

But while you ought highly to estimate the privilege
of good society as a means of forming your manners,
you cannot too cautiously guard against servile imitation.   You may have a friend whose manners seem to
you to combine every quality that is necessary to render them a perfect model; who unites elegant simplicity with generous frankness, and dignified address
with winning condescension; who, in short, is every
thing, in this respect, that you could wish to be yourself; but after all, it would be unwise in you to become
a servile copyist even of such manners.   For you are
to remember, that a certain cast of manners suits a
certain cast of character; and unless your character
were precisely that of the individual whom you should
imitate, you would, in attempting to assume her address, deservedly expose yourself to the charge of
affectation.   You will therefore do yourself much better service by looking at good models in a general
manner, and by endeavoring to become imbued with
their spirit, than by making any direct efforts to become exactly conformed to them.   Indeed, it may be
doubted whether you will not reap every possible advantage by simply mingling in their society, without
even thinking of them as models.

Let me caution you here more particularly to be

on your guard against affectation. This is very easily acquired, and is so common a fault, that the absence of it is always remarked as a great excellence. I have known females of many amiable qualities, and considerable intelligence, who have been absolutely spoiled for society by attempting to assume in their manners what did not belong to them. Wherever any thing of this kind exists, it requires but little sagacity to detect it; and even those who are not exactly sensible where the evil lies, are still aware that there is something which needs to be corrected. It happens however, too frequently, that what is quite palpable to every body else escapes the observation of the individual who is the subject of it; and I have known glaring cases, in which the kindest intimation of the fact, from a friend, has been met with expressions of resentment. I beg that you will not only have your ears open to any admonition you may ever receive on this subject, but your eyes open, to inspect narrowly your own conduct, that you may detect the fault if it really exists. It is always regarded, and justly regarded, as an indication of consummate folly; and unless it happens to be associated with an unusual cluster of real excellences, it brings upon the individual little less than absolute contempt. Let your manners be as much improved as they may, but regard it as an essential matter that they should be your own.

Beware also of an ostentatious manner. By this I mean that kind of manner which savors too much of

display; which indicates a disposition to make yourself too conspicuous; and which, in short, is the acting
out of a spirit of self-confidence and self-conceit. This
appears badly enough when discovered in a man; but
in a female, and especially in a young female, it is absolutely intolerable. Not that I wish to see you awk-
wardly bashful, or liable to embarrassment from every
slight change of circumstances; but between this and
the ostentatious manner which I am condemning, there
is a happy medium consisting of a due mixture of confidence and modesty, which will be equally pleasant to
yourself and those with whom you associate. But if
you must err on either extreme, I had rather it would
be on that of diffidence than of ostentation. I had
rather you should excite, by your bashfulness, a feeling of compassion, than by your excessive confidence
a feeling of disgust.

But while you are carefully to avoid ostentation,
you are to guard with no less caution against a studied
reserve. We sometimes meet with persons whose
manners leave upon our minds the painful impression
that they are afraid to trust us; and that they regard
both our actions and words with suspicion. Wherever
this trait appears, it is almost certain to excite anger
or disgust. Most persons will bear any thing with
more patience than to be told, either directly or indirectly, that they are unworthy of confidence. A sig-
nificant smile, or nod, or look, with a third person,
which is intended not to be understood by the individ-

ual with whom you are conversing, is a gross violation of propriety, and has often cost a deeply wounded sensibility, and sometimes a valued friendship. While you studiously avoid every thing of this kind, let your manners be characterized by a noble frankness, which, in whatever circumstances you are placed, shall leave no doubt of your sincerity.

I will only add, that you should avoid every approach to a haughty and overbearing manner. I would fain indulge the hope that your feelings will be an effectual security against this most offensive characteristic; but be that as it may, I assure you that you can never exhibit it, but at an expense of reputation which you can ill afford to incur. It is an exhibition of pride, which is one of the most hateful of all dispositions; and of pride in one of its most odious forms. If you should be so unhappy as to furnish an example of it, whatever variety of feeling it might excite among your superiors and equals and inferiors, you may rely on it they would all agree to despise you. I entreat you, therefore, as you value your character or usefulness, that you will always be courteous and condescending. It is the mark of a truly noble disposition to be able to treat the most menial and dependent with kindness and good will.

If I should point you to the finest model of female manners which it has ever been my privilege to observe, and one which will compare with the most perfect models of this or any other age, I should repeat a

venerated name which I have already had occasion to
mention in another connection—that of Mrs. Hannah
More.   It was my privilege, a few years ago, while
on a tour through England for health, to make a
visit at the residence of this distinguished female—a
visit which I have ever since regarded as among the
happiest incidents of my life.   At that time she num-
bered more than fourscore years, but the vigor of her
intellect was scarcely at all impaired ; and from what
she was, I could easily conceive what she had been
when her sun was at its meridian.   In her person she
was rather small, but was a specimen of admirable
symmetry.   In her manners she united the dignity
and refinement of the court, with the most exquisite
urbanity and gentleness which the female character
in its loveliest forms ever exhibited.   She impressed
me continually with a sense of the high intellectual
and moral qualities by which she was distinguished,
but still left me as unconstrained as if I had been conversing with my beloved child.   There was an air of
graceful and unaffected ease, an instinctive regard to
the most delicate proprieties of social intercourse, a
readiness to communicate, and yet a desire to listen,
the dignity of conscious merit united with the humility
of the devoted Christian ; in short, there was such an
assemblage of intellectual and moral excellences beam-
ing forth in every expression and look and attitude,
that I could scarcely conceive of a more perfect exhibition of human character.   I rejoice that it is your

privilege to know Mrs. More through her works; and I can form no better wish for you than that you may imbibe her spirit, and according to your humble measure, walk in her footsteps.

I am, with earnest prayers for your happiness,

Your affectionate

FATHER.

LETTER IX.

CONVERSATION.

My dear Child—In the preceding letter I have given you some general directions in respect to the formation of your manners. The subject on which I am now to address you is closely connected with that; but yet, if I mistake not, is sufficiently distinct to justify a consideration of it in a separate letter.

I am well aware that the gift of conversation is originally possessed in very unequal measures; and that while some have a native aptitude for social intercourse, others seem to be constitutionally deficient in ease and fluency. But notwithstanding this original diversity, there is perhaps no talent that is more susceptible of improvement than the talent for conversation; and though you should possess it in ever so moderate a degree, you may still, by a suitable degree of attention, render yourself, in this respect, decent and respectable.

The first requisite for conversing well, is a well-stored and cultivated mind. Without this, I acknowledge that you may talk fluently, and talk abundantly,

and if you please, talk humorously ; but you can never
be qualified to hold your part to advantage in intelligent social intercourse.   If you move in the walks
of cultivated society, you will find that a great variety
of topics will come up, beyond the mere common-
places of the day ; and unless you have become considerably conversant with the various departments of
knowledge, you will be subjected to the mortification
of betraying your ignorance either by saying nothing,
or by saying that which is not to the purpose.   There
is no subject of importance, the slightest knowledge of
which may not be of advantage to you in conversation ;
for even though it should be too limited to enable you
to impart any thing to those with whom you converse,
it may be of great use in assisting you to prosecute
your inquiries with intelligence, and thus to increase
your own stock of information.   I would say then, be
studious to gain knowledge on every important subject,
and do not regard even the fragments of information
as too unimportant to be treasured up and retained.

Endeavor, as far as possible, to make your conversation a source of improvement.   The gift of speech,
like every other endowment, was bestowed for an important purpose ; and that purpose can never be
answered, unless it is made the vehicle for communicating, or the means of obtaining useful knowledge or
good impressions.   See then that you use this invalu-
able gift as not abusing it.   Wherever it is in your
power to command the conversation, make it a primary

object to give it such a turn that it shall subserve the intellectual and moral advantage of those who are engaged in it.   It may be well for you, with reference to your own improvement, to endeavor to introduce such topics as may best suit the taste or talents of those with whom you converse—topics upon which they will be most at home, and will be most likely to throw out thoughts that may be useful to you.   It has often happened that an individual, from one conversation with an intelligent friend, has gained more light on a particular subject, than would have been gained by weeks or even months of reading or reflection. And let me say, there are scarcely any circumstances in which you can be placed, in which you may not render the conversation a source of some advantage, either to yourself or others.   If you are thrown among the illiterate and vulgar, you may, in a single half hour, do something to enlighten them ; you may even be instrumental in giving a new direction to their thoughts, and ultimately of forming their character in a better mould : and notwithstanding their ignorance on most subjects, there may be some on which they may be able to instruct you ; and thus, after all, you may be mutually benefited by your intercourse.   Not a small part of the sins of almost every individual are sins of the tongue.   If you keep in view what ought to be the great end of conversation, it will secure you, in a good degree, against this whole class of offences.

Let me caution you to beware of talking too much.

If you do not talk to the purpose, the less you say the better ; but even if you do, and if withal, you are gifted with the best powers of conversation, it will be wise for you to guard against the imputation of excessive loquacity.   I would not by any means have you yield to a prudish reserve ; but I know not whether even that were a more offensive extreme than to monopolize the conversation of a whole circle.   You are to remember that as the gift of speech is common to all, so there are few who are not inclined to use it ; and it is a rare case, indeed, that you will meet an individual who will feel satisfied to sit down and hear another talk continually, and have the conversation addressed to himself, without bearing any part in it. But at any rate, you are never to make yourself very conspicuous in conversation, without due regard to circumstances.   If, for instance, you are among persons who are your superiors in age or standing in society, there must be strong circumstances to justify you in bearing more than a moderate share in the conversation.   And if you should actually take the lead in it, let it appear manifest that it is not because you are predisposed to do so, but because it is the wish of others that you should.   If you talk out of proportion to your relative circumstances, even though it should be to the amusement or edification of those who listen, it is more than probable that it will be set down to the score of vanity.   It were far better to leave a circle wishing, from what you have actually said, that

you had said more, than out of patience with you for
having talked so much.

It is only an extension of the thought to which I
have just adverted, when I remark further, that you
should beware of talking without reflection, or when
you have nothing to say.   It is far better to be silent
than to talk in this manner, or in these circumstances ;
for you cannot hope to edify any one, and you certainly expose yourself.   Let the subject be what it
may, accustom yourself always to reflect before you
speak ; in other words, to have thoughts before you
utter them.   You cannot look around in society, without perceiving that incautious speaking is one of the
most fruitful sources of mischief.   Whether you are
discussing a grave subject, or talking about the most
familiar occurrences of life, let it be a rule from which
you never deviate, to say nothing without reflection.
You may easily form this habit, and the advantage of
it will be incalculable ; or you may perhaps, with still
greater ease, form the opposite habit, and it will not
improbably subject you to serious evils as long as you
live.

Take care that you never subject yourself to the
charge of egotism.   This is apt to be a consequence of
excessive garrulity ; for there are few persons who talk
a great deal, that do not find it convenient to magnify
their own importance.   And let me say that this is a
foible which is more likely to escape the observation
of the person who is subject to it, than almost any

other; and yet there is perhaps no other which by every one else is more easily detected; and I may add, none which excites more universal disgust. Guard your lips, then, whenever you find it in your heart to make yourself the heroine of your own story.

Never say any thing of yourself which even indirectly involves commendation, unless under circumstances of very rare occurrence. If you watch the operations of your heart, you will probably be surprised to find how strong is the propensity to bring one's self into view, as often and to as great advantage as possible. Whenever you can illustrate any subject on which you may be conversing by a reference to the experience of any one else, it is better, in all ordinary cases, to avail yourself of it, than to refer even indirectly to your own. I have known some persons, who have manifested a strange kind of egotism, in speaking freely and unnecessarily of their own past errors, when it appeared to me that genuine humility would have led them to silent communion with their hearts, and penitence before God. You may rest assured that it is an exceedingly difficult thing to allude much either to one's own faults or excellences—difficult, I mean, without leaving an impression that it is the offspring of a foolish self-complacency; in other words, without getting, and deservedly getting the character of an egotist.

Avoid even the appearance of pedantry. If you are conversing with persons of very limited attainments, you will make yourself far more acceptable as well as useful to them, by accommodating yourself to their capacities, than by compelling them to listen to what they cannot understand. I do not say that you may not in some instances make them stare at your supposed wisdom, and perhaps they may even quote you as an oracle of learning; but it is much more probable that even they will smile at such an exhibition as a contemptible weakness. With the intelligent and discerning, this effect certainly will be produced; and that whether your pretensions to learning are well founded or not: the simple fact that you aim to appear learned, that you deal much in allusions to the classics or the various departments of science, with an evident intention to display your familiarity with them, will be more intolerable than even absolute ignorance. If you are really a proficient in science or literature, you need have no apprehensions that your acquisitions will not be known without your making a formal proclamation of them. If you are only a superficial student, and make pretensions to learning which your acquirements do not justify, you will inevitably have to encounter a mortifying defeat; for you may set it down that in cultivated society you will pass for nothing more than you are really worth. My advice to you is, to acquire as much useful information as you can, and to use it in conversation where there is manifestly occasion for it; but in no case whatever to volunteer a learned remark where there is no higher purpose to be answered than mere personal display. And never venture on a subject, especially with an air of confidence and erudition, upon which you are conscious your attainments are too shallow to justify it. It is an experiment always fraught with danger; and many instances have I known in which it has resulted in a humiliating exposure both of ignorance and weakness. You are at liberty, indeed, to converse upon subjects on which you are not well informed: this, as I have elsewhere intimated, is one important means of increasing your information; but, in every such case, do not attempt to get more credit for intelligence than you really deserve: do not assume the air of a teacher when you are conscious that the attitude of a learner belongs to you. In this respect, as well as in every other, honesty is the safest and best policy.

Let me caution you still further against a habit of light conversation. I have known young females with whom this habit had become so confirmed, that it seemed as if they could scarcely speak but to trifle; and who would even choose to remain silent, rather than join in conversation in which their favorite passion could not be indulged. You cannot contract such a habit but at the expense of forfeiting the esteem of the wise and good, of sacrificing true dignity of character, and throwing yourself into a current of temptation in which there is every probability that you will be irrecoverably lost. Scarcely any habit more effectually than this imparts a disrelish for the society of all ex-

cept triflers, and hardens the heart against the influences of religion. I do not wish ever to see you
gloomy, or austere, or spiritless; but as you value all
that is most precious in time and eternity, I pray you
never to give yourself up to a habit of levity. Avoid
even the most distant approach to it; for it is the
nature of every habit, and especially of this, to make
an insidious beginning, and to grow strong by indulgence. If you are thrown into company in which
it is the fashion to trifle, get out of it as soon as possible; and while you are in it, have decision enough to
let it appear that you are not in your favorite element;
and if you should even have so much as to express
your disapprobation, and to administer a gentle yet
dignified reproof, I venture to say, that the greatest
trifler in the circle would respect you the more for it.
There is no apology to be made for such a habit on
the ground of constitution, education, or any thing
else; and if you yield to it, I must again remind you
that you do it at the expense of character, usefulness,
happiness, and heaven.

Be careful also how you indulge in sarcasm. If
you are constitutionally inclined to this, you will find
that there is no point in your character which needs
to be more faithfully guarded. There are some few
cases in which severe irony may be employed to advantage—cases in which vice and error will shrink
before it, when they will unhesitatingly confront every
other species of opposition. But it too often happens

that those who possess this talent use it too indiscriminately; and perhaps even more frequently to confound
modest and retiring virtue, than to abash bold and
insolent vice. But be assured that it is a contemptible triumph that is gained, when, by the force of sarcasm, the lips of a deserving individual are sealed, and
the countenance crimsoned with blushes. And there
are only a few cases—cases in which the cast of character is peculiar—that will warrant the use of this weapon
against vice itself. You may take it for granted, in
all ordinary cases in which a sarcastic remark has done
its office, that you have excited feelings of no very
friendly character towards yourself. You may be
flattered by the compliment which you imagine those
around you are paying to your wit, but it were more
reasonable for you to grieve at the reflection that you
have not improbably lost a friend.

In connection with sarcasm as displayed towards
those with whom you converse, let me say a word in
respect to your treatment of absent characters. Never
volunteer unnecessarily in speaking ill of any body.
You may indeed be placed in circumstances in which
it may be proper, and even necessary, that you should
express an unfavorable opinion of characters—that
you should state facts concerning them of the most
disagreeable nature. But what I object to is, that
you should do this when circumstances do not require
it, and when no good will be likely to result from it;
for it at once indicates a bad disposition, and is a

means by which that disposition will gain strength.
But in no case allow yourself to make any unfavorable
representation of a character, unless you have ample
evidence that it is accordant with truth.   By neglecting to observe this direction, you may do an injury to
an innocent person, which it will afterwards never be
in your power to retrieve ; and withal, you may acquire
for yourself the reputation of a slanderer.   There is
an idle way of discussing characters, in which less is
usually meant than meets the ear, and which often
seems to be resorted to merely for the sake of filling
up the time.   Remember that if you allow yourself to
join in this kind of conversation, you always do it at
the hazard of making for yourself enemies ; for though
your remarks may be made with perfectly harmless
intentions, and may convey no bad impressions to the
individual to whom they are addressed, yet when they
reach the ear of the person who is the subject of them,
unaccompanied by the manner in which they were
uttered, and not improbably in an exaggerated form,
they will almost of course be regarded as indicating
diminished friendship, if not decided hostility.   Above
all, never venture censorious remarks upon characters
when you are thrown among strangers.   Many instances have occurred in which an individual who has
ventured upon this experiment, has afterwards made
the mortifying discovery that the person who was the
subject of his remarks was listening to them ; or if not,
that they were heard by some near relative or friend.

The only prudent course in such circumstances, is to say nothing which will expose your own feelings or the feelings of others in view of any disclosure that may be made.

There is a familiar and irreverent use of sacred things, against which I wish especially to guard you. For a female to be absolutely profane, would be to render herself at once an outlaw from decent society; nevertheless, I have observed with pain that some young ladies, who would doubtless shrink from the charge of profaneness, allow themselves in exclamations, and in irreverent and ludicrous applications of Scripture, which border very closely upon it. Beware how you even approach this dangerous ground. Such exclamations as those to which I have referred, in which either the awful name of the Supreme Being or some one of his attributes is lightly introduced, are fitted to destroy your reverence for every thing sacred, and to cherish within you a spirit of absolute impiety. Never suffer any thing of a sacred nature to be on your lips, without a corresponding sentiment of reverence in your heart. And if those with whom you are accustomed to associate indulge themselves in this inconsiderate habit of which I have spoken, think it a sufficient reason for declining their society; for certain it is, that you can gain nothing from it to compensate the loss which you would be liable to sustain of your reverence for the character or word of God.

I will only detain you further by suggesting a

caution to cherish a most sacred regard to truth.   It
would give me great pain to suppose for a moment
that, at the age to which you have now arrived, you
should ever be guilty of deliberate falsehood; but I
wish to put you on your guard against every thing
that has even the semblance of a disregard to strict
veracity.   There is a habit which many persons have
of dealing artfully and evasively; saving their con-
sciences by some expression which may admit of
double construction, but which nevertheless in its obvious construction is contrary to truth.   There are
others who have a habit of talking extravagantly on
every subject; with whom the simple verity is too
dry to be relished; who suffer their imaginations to
supply the defects of their memories; who, in short,
never seem to breathe freely but in the region of em-
bellishment and exaggeration.   And I am constrained
to say that much of the civility of fashionable life
savors strongly of deception.   I refer here not only to
the habit which some ladies have of sending word to
visitors that they are not at home, when they are only
engaged, but to the painful regrets that are often expressed at the distance between calls—at the unspeak-
able joy which is manifested on meeting a fashionable
acquaintance—at the earnest importunity that is exhibited for an early visit, when the truth is in each
case that the real feeling is that of absolute indifference.   Now I beg you will guard against duplicity in
all its forms.   Rely on it, it is not necessary to true

politeness; and if it were, you ought not, as an accountable and immortal creature, even to agitate the question whether you shall yield to it. There are cases, I know, in which the temptation to equivocate is powerful, in which to speak the honest truth must involve severe personal sacrifices; but in all cases of this kind the only proper alternative is, either to speak out your real sentiments, or to say nothing; and you are not even at liberty to remain silent, when silence will convey a wrong impression, and of course is virtual falsehood. You will gain nothing if you allow yourself in a habit of exaggeration; for this feature in your character will soon be understood, and your statements will all be received with a corresponding abatement. In a word, let it be a principle with you never to be violated, that in whatever circumstances you are placed, all that you say shall be characterized by the simplicity of truth. Mrs. Opie's "Illustrations of Lying" is a work adapted to lead you to an intimate knowledge of the windings of your own heart, or to put you on your guard against the beginning of this evil.

Your

FATHER.

LETTER X.

AMUSEMENTS.

My dear Child—There is scarcely any subject on which it is more important that you should form correct notions, and in relation to which a mistaken view is of more practical and dangerous tendency, than that of amusements. Many a young female, who might have been an ornament to her sex, and a blessing to the world, has, by yielding to the dictates of a wayward inclination, and setting aside the decisions of sober reason on this subject, not only rendered herself of no account in society, but clouded all her prospects both for this world and another. In contemplating this subject, I wish you to feel that you are standing by the grave of female character and hopes, and to heed the monitory voice that issues from it, charging you to beware how you tread in the footsteps of the fallen and ruined.

The grand reason why so many females have fallen victims to the love of amusement is, that they have judged erroneously of the end which it is designed to answer. They have taken up the opinion, and it must

be acknowledged that it has too often received the
sanction even of parents, that a portion especially of
early life was designed to be frittered away in idle and
foolish indulgences; that they are at liberty during
this period to regard the gratification of the senses as
an ultimate object, and to think of nothing in connection with amusement beyond the mere momentary
enjoyment with which it is connected. With this impression they have asked no question with so much
interest as how they may most effectually be amused;
and this passion has increased by indulgence, until
they have acquired an utter disrelish for the sober
concerns of life. Who would suppose that beings
could be employed in these idle pursuits, who are
destined to an immortal existence, who are accountable for the improvement of all their time, and are liable
every hour to enter on an exact and eternal retribution?

The only rational view of this subject is that which
takes for granted our obligation to use all our faculties
at all times to the best purpose. This is a first principle not only of Scripture, but of reason; and it were
impossible to prove that we are exempt from this obligation a single moment, by any argument which would
not at the same time prove that we are always exempt
from it—in other words, which would not disprove
human accountableness and sweep away the pillars of
God's moral government. It is a command, dictated
by God's own Spirit, that whatever we do we should
do all to his glory; and if there had been any depart-

ment of human action to which this command was not designed to extend, it were impossible but that the exception should have been made. The legitimate end of amusement therefore is not answered in mere personal gratification, but in refreshing and invigorating the powers for the more successful discharge of duty. The constitution of the human mind is such, that it will not bear to be intensely employed on the same object for a long time without interruption: the effect of an attempt to keep it thus employed would be, that far less would be accomplished than might be with occasional relaxation; and withal, the energies of the mind, instead of being quickened and improved, would gradually be diminished. Hence some amusement becomes necessary, in order to secure the greatest usefulness.

In this view, you will perceive not only that amusement is designed to prepare you for the discharge of duty, that is, for an attention to the graver concerns of life, but that it is itself an important part of duty, and like every thing else in which you engage, ought to be subject to the direction of conscience. You have no more right to forget your accountableness or to refuse to acknowledge God in selecting your amusements, or in yielding yourself to them, than you have when you enter the closet or sanctuary to engage in private or public worship.

You will perceive, moreover, if the preceding remarks are correct, that the whole purpose of amuse-

ment may be answered by mere change of employment.
It is by no means necessary, as the popular notion is,
that the change should be from an employment that
is useful to one that is useless or even worse ; but the
object may be even better accomplished by a change
that shall keep the mind still employed to advantage.
of your ordinary employment is one that lays your
faculties under severe contribution, that to which you
resort for amusement ought undoubtedly to require
but moderate mental exercise ; and in cases of great
exhaustion from intellectual effort, it may be proper
to give the mind for a season an entire dispensation
from the labor of connected thought. But in all
ordinary cases, you will find that in unbending from
severe exertion of mind, with reference to renewing
that exertion with greater success, you need not yield
to positive inaction, or occupy yourself with any thing
that is trifling, but may still be doing something for
the benefit of yourself or your fellow-creatures. If
you regulate your amusements by a regard to this
principle, you will find it a most effectual means of
redeeming time, and will have the pleasure to reflect
that even your hours of relaxation are hours of usefulness.

There are several tests by which you may judge
whether any particular amusement is innocent; of
course, whether it is safe and right for you to indulge
in it. Inquire, for instance, whether, before engaging
in it, you dare enter your closet and ask God to ac-

company it with his blessing. Do not think this a superstitious suggestion. Rely on it, it is fully accordant with enlightened reason and conscience. We have no right to use our faculties in any way which our Maker and Judge does not approve; and if we are conscious of using them aright, we shall at once feel our need of his blessing, and be encouraged to supplicate it. I am well aware that it is a thought which has never entered the mind of most young persons, that God should be acknowledged in their amusements; and if they have ever thought of attempting to approach this awful and glorious Being, this has been a subject on which conscience has dictated petitions for forgiveness, though the idea of supplicating a blessing would seem to them little short of impiety. The reason obviously is, that the amusements in which they indulge are felt to be wrong: they are not such as will abide the scrutiny of an enlightened conscience, much less the scrutiny of a holy God. If you dare not enter your closet and ask God to bless you in any amusement in which you are about to engage, you may safely take that as a testimony of conscience against it; and if you do not retreat, you may make up your mind to encounter the lashes of conscience hereafter, as part of your retribution for disobeying her suggestions.

Equally certain is it that it cannot be right to engage in any amusement which is fitted to give you a disrelish for serious reflection. All who acknowledge the truth of the Bible, indeed all but the downright atheist, are compelléd to admit that the circumstances of our present existence are deeply solemn ; and that he who shuts his eyes against them is chargeable with gross infatuation. We are here passing the only period of our probation for eternity. The glories of immortal life are brought within our reach, and are suspended on our acceptance of the terms of the gospel ; and the very first step towards the acceptance of these terms, is serious consideration. Is it not manifest then, that any thing which excites a disrelish for reflection, and of course puts at hazard the soul's everlasting interests, must be wrong? If you find that such has been the effect of any amusement in which you have indulged, let it be a reason why you should instantly abandon it : or if you are convinced that such would be the effect of any to which you are solicited or inclined, let it be a reason why you stand aloof from it, and maintain your ground with unyielding firmness.

It were preposterous, moreover, to practise any amusement which you cannot think of without pain or remorse, in connection with the prospect of dying. That death is the certain lot of all, and of yourself in common with others, is a fact just as well established as the fact of your existence. That death itself is a most serious event, and that the consequences connected with it are momentous beyond our conceptions, is no matter of question with any believer in divine revelation. Equally certain is it, that the hour of our

departure from this world may be rendered the peace-
ful dawn of an eternal day, or it may be an hour of
darkness and agitation and horror which the boldest
imagination cannot describe.   Now I ask again, is it
not more than madness to engage in any amusement
which conscience tells you will not bear to be reviewed
when the current of life is ebbing away ; nay, which
must inevitably plant a thorn in your dying pillow?
Surely no person who acts under the influence of
reason can object to this, as a perfectly fair test by
which to decide upon the guilt or innocence of any
amusement ; for no one can deny, that it is the dictate
of true wisdom that we should consider and prepare
for our latter end.   Here then I pray you to take
counsel of reason, and not suffer yourself to be deluded
by mere feeling ; and if you are tempted to amuse
yourself in any way which you really believe will cast
an additional shade upon the dark valley, or the tendency of which is to make you wish that death were
more distant, resist the temptation, let it be at whatever expense it may.   There is no worldly gratification which it were not wise to forego, if it be a seed
which will yield a harvest of wretchedness in your last
hour.

Let me add, that you cannot innocently indulge in
any amusement which will not fit you for the better
discharge of the ordinary duties of life.   If this be not
the effect, the time which is thus occupied is worse
than lost ; for not only is there no good accomplished,

but the faculties, by this means, acquire, or are confirmed in a wrong direction. And thus habits are
often formed, both intellectual and moral, which are
alike inconsistent with dignity, happiness, and usefulness. But surely I need not again remind you that,
in respect to the improvement of your time, and the
use of your faculties, you are a steward of God; and
that you cannot be indifferent concerning either, but
at the expense of proving yourself unfaithful, and of
incurring the Master's displeasure. Is it not lamenta-
bly true, that a large part of the amusements that
prevail in the world, instead of invigorating the faculties for the more faithful discharge of duty, actually
unfit the mind for useful exertion on the one hand, and
create a disrelish for it on the other? I need not repeat the caution that you will have no communion
with any of these scenes of unprofitable indulgence.

That you may not misapprehend my meaning, I will
descend a little to particulars, and give you my opinion, in a few words, of some of the fashionable amusements of the day.

I will begin with parties of pleasure. You already
know that I am in favor of your cultivating the social
affections. Instead of objecting to your meeting occasionally a circle of friends, for an agreeable interchange of kind sentiments, and for purposes of intellectual and moral improvement, I would encourage
such meetings with all my heart; and if you choose to
call them parties of pleasure, you have my consent for

doing so. But those scenes which usually pass in the world under this name—scenes of mere conviviality and trifling—in which there is nothing to enlighten the mind, or to refine or elevate the affections, I am constrained to regard as utterly unworthy a rational and accountable being. It is not the fact that the occasions to which I refer usually collect a large number, that constitutes the ground of my objection to them; for a large number may as well be occupied in a profitable manner as a small one; but it is the fact that the very purpose for which they come together is to fritter away time in idle and foolish conversation. It is this circumstance which gives to the parties to which I refer their distinctive character; and whether they consist of many or few, their tendency is perhaps equally pernicious. They not only answer no good purpose, but serve to dissipate the mind, and throw open the doors of the heart to every temptation.

Another amusement which has been very common, and which still prevails to a considerable extent. is dancing. To this, considered as a mere exercise, no objection certainly can be made; and if it were culti-vated with exclusive reference to this, nothing worse could be said of learning to dance, than that it is not the most profitable way of spending time. And I will go further and add, that if a few girls were disposed to stand up together for a half hour, and dance for recreation, I cannot conceive that there could be any immorality in it. But all this, you are perfectly aware, is very remote from the amusement as it actually exists. Every one knows that it brings the sexes together in circumstances, to say the least, not the most favorable to the cultivation of female delicacy; that the mind is usually engrossed for a considerable time, in preparation for it; that, for the most part, it occupies hours which the Creator designed should be given to repose; that it is fitted to cherish a spirit of vanity, and work up the mind to a feverish and useless excitement; and that it is followed by a state, both of mind and body, which, for a time at least, forbids any thing like useful exertion. I am confident that I might appeal to any young female who is accustomed to dance in balls and assemblies, and if she were honest, she would confirm, from her own experience, all that I have said. I have been struck with the fact that in every instance in which I have ever heard a young female, under serious impressions, speak of that part of her life which she has devoted to this amusement, she has said, unhesitatingly, that, more than any thing else, it served to confirm her in a habit of carelessness, and to give her an aversion to the concerns of religion. Such testimony rendered in such circumstances, ought surely to be regarded as decisive.

The only other amusement in relation to which I shall at present offer an opinion, is the theatre. The great argument which is urged in favor of this is, that it is a school in which you may study to advantage the human character; inasmuch as the various operations of the heart, under different circumstances, are here successfully exhibited. This argument is worth nothing; for it were better to study human nature, as it is acted out in the every-day realities of life around us, than as it appears in the high-wrought and over-strained representations of the stage; just as it would be desirable to contemplate any object of interest, rather than a picture of it, even though it might be drawn by the most skilful artist. And as for the objections to this amusement, they are so obvious that I scarcely need allude to them. The vulgarity, the licentiousness, the impiety connected with it, are pro-verbial; and if the fact did not stare us in the face, we should say that it was impossible that ladies pro-fessing the utmost delicacy, and who, in private, would be offended by an indecent allusion, will nevertheless deliberately and habitually expose themselves to all the profaneness and ribaldry of the stage. And what renders this still more surprising is, that in being pres-ent on these occasions, they consent to mingle with the most profligate part of the community—with persons who are at home only in the atmosphere of moral cor-ruption, and whom common decency cannot behold without a blush. I say this is a fact in the history of your sex, for which I own myself utterly unable to ac-count; but I earnestly hope that I may never be com-pelled to contemplate an example of it in my own child. Should this be the case, I should consider my fond hopes in respect to you as blasted, and should shed tears of deeper anguish than if I had consigned you to an early grave.

If the thought should occur to you that I am abridging your liberty too far, by depriving you of amusements which are regarded by many as innocent, let me entreat you, before you indulge such a reflection, to pause and refer the several species of amusement of which I have spoken, to the tests which I am sure your reason and conscience have already approved. Upon which of them, let me ask, could you, in your closet, and upon your knees, humbly invoke the blessing of God? Which of them could you indulge, and not feel an increased aversion to the serious concerns of religion; especially to the duty of self-examination, and communion with God? In which of them should you be willing to engage, if you were to be assured by a messenger from the invisible world, that you were spending the last month or the last week of your probation. In relation to which of them can you say, in the presence of the Searcher of hearts, that it would serve to prepare you the better for the various personal and relative duties of life? I am sure that I need only propose these interrogatories to your conscience, to satisfy you that there is no superstition in the advice which I have given you in respect to these several amusements.

But I know you will ask, if the fashionable amusements of the day are proscribed, what are those in which you may safely and innocently indulge. I answer in general by repeating what I have already said, that there is scarcely any employment, different from your ordinary one, which requires comparatively little mental effort, in which you may not find legitimate recreation. You may amuse yourself by various kinds of reading, which at the same time will exert a favorable influence on your understanding and heart. You may amuse yourself by the study of natural science; especially by arranging the flowers of the field, and calling them by their names; or by carrying your curious researches into the mineral kingdom, and decyphering the evidences of the Creator's handiwork in the mountain rock, and the insignificant pebble, and every degree of mineral existence between them. You may amuse yourself by cheerful and yet useful conversation with some entertaining friend, or even by walking abroad in solitude, and breathing the fresh air, and looking at the moon and the stars as they shine forth in silent grandeur on the face of the sky, or in contemplating the bright verdure that covers the earth in spring, or in listening to the sound of a distant brook, as it rushes down a steep mountain and buries itself in a deep forest. The contemplation of these various objects, and of all the variegated scenery of nature, opens a most legitimate field for amusement, while it is fitted also to enlarge our conceptions of the Creator's works, and to foster a spirit of elevated devotion and rational piety.

I am your affectionate

FATHER.

LETTER XI.

INTERCOURSE WITH THE WORLD.

My dear Child—In several of the preceding letters I have taken for granted that you are to mingle, in a greater or less degree, in society. It is equally essential to your respectability and usefulness, that you should not live the life of a recluse. The constitution of your nature, and the circumstances of your condition clearly indicate that you were made to be social. As it is a subject, however, in relation to which there is a strong tendency to extremes, and on which you will be in great danger of being misled, I shall suggest a few thoughts in the present letter, which may serve to aid in forming your opinions and directing your conduct.

I begin my advice to you on this subject by a caution that you should not make your entrance into society at too early a period. It too often happens that girls, long before they have completed their education, and even at a comparatively early stage of it, have contracted a strong relish for being in the world ; and unless prevented by the influence of parents or instructors, they are found thus prematurely in the gayest circles of fashion. The consequence of this is, that at best a divided attention is rendered to their studies; that their opportunities for intellectual improvement are enjoyed to little purpose; and that the period in which should be laid the foundation of a solid and useful character, is perverted to the formation of a habit of mental inaction, and not improbably to cherish a spirit of intolerable vanity.

Now I do not insist that you should actually decline all society up to the time of completing your education; but I wish that your visiting, previous to that period, should be, for the most part, of an informal character; and that you should not generally consider yourself at liberty to accept invitations, even if you should receive them, to mingle in set circles. This accidental intercourse of which I have spoken, is all that will be necessary during the period of your education, to aid you in the formation of your manners; and any thing beyond it will almost inevitably interfere with your intellectual improvement, and of course detract from your ultimate standing in society.

Let me assure you too, that you will be far less acceptable in society, if you make your appearance prematurely, than if you wait till a proper period. The common-sense of the world is quick to discern any impropriety on this subject; and if while you are yet a child, you are seen among those of mature age, virtually claiming to be as old as they, you can expect nothing else but that you will be set down as deficient either in modesty or good sense. Better for your reputation that you should come too late into society than too early; for though in the one case you might lose something in point of manners, yet in the other you would lose more, in the estimation of the world, on the score of delicacy and correct judgment.

It is not more important that you should avoid going into society too early, than it is, that when you do enter it, you should avoid mingling in it too much. One bad effect of this would be, that it would leave you with too little time for the discharge of your private and domestic duties. The culture of your mind and heart, in connection with the ordinary cares of domestic life, requires that a large part of your time should be spent at home; and you cannot, without great injustice to yourself, and those with whom you are connected, neglect these more private duties, for the sake of being always in the bustle of the world. It is a rare thing that you will find a lady who devotes an undue proportion of her time to visiting, but if you follow her into the domestic circle, to the chamber and the fireside, you will find that she evinces a proportional neglect of some of the duties belonging to the station she occupies. She is either neglecting to cultivate her understanding, or neglecting to keep her heart, or neglecting to use the means which Providence has put into her hands for the intellectual and moral improvement of those with whom she is immediately connected.

Recollect also, that the error against which I am

endeavoring to put you on your guard, would not only prevent your attention to more important duties, by occupying the time which should be allotted to them, but it would serve actually to give you a distaste for those duties. Allow yourself in a constant round of company, even for a short period, and it will be strange indeed, if you do not begin to feel that company is your only element—if you do not, in a great degree, lose your relish for the pleasures of the domestic fireside—if you do not find yourself complaining of ennui, when you happen for a season to be providentially shut up at home. I need not stop to show how entirely such a habit of feeling must disqualify a female for the most important relations she can ever sustain.

Moreover, an extravagant fondness for society, and an excessive indulgence of this inclination, are almost sure to create a habit of dissipation, both as it respects the intellect and the feelings. The mind, by being constantly conversant with the ever varying scenes of social life, loses, in a great degree, the command of its own powers ; and the attempt to concentrate them on any particular subject were scarcely more likely to succeed, than would be an attempt to collect every mote that was floating in the surrounding atmosphere, while the atmosphere was agitated by a whirlwind. The moral feelings too are subject to a similar influence ; for not only is there usually an entire absence of self-communion, and all that secret discipline of the affections, which is essential to the right keeping of the heart, but too often there are the levities of the world, scenes from which there is a studied exclusion of religion, and even a designed introduction of much that is fitted to bring religion into contempt. I do not say that this evil, in its whole extent, is commonly found in any of the walks of decent society; but I do say that it sometimes exists in the frightful dimensions which I have attributed to it; and that it commonly exists in so great a degree as to render an excessive intercourse with the world a fruitful source of mischief.

You will anticipate me when I say, in this connection, that it becomes you to use the utmost caution in selecting the circle with which you are to associate. I hardly need admonish you to set it down as a fixed purpose, that you will never intentionally be found in any circle in which there is any thing to encourage immorality, or any lack of reverence for the sacred principles and precepts of religion. I would have you, moreover, beware of mingling in the gay world—in scenes which are designed to produce an unnatural and feverish excitement of the spirits, which are fraught with no intellectual or moral advantage, and in which the introduction of grave or useful discourse would be the signal for disquietude or disgust. I do not, by any means, insist that your associates should all be from the number of those who are professedly or actually pious; nor do I object at all to your intercourse with them being of a cheerful, and sometimes, if you please, an amusing character; but I do insist that they should be persons of correct moral views and habits, and that your associating with them should be for some higher purpose than merely to kill time, or to cultivate a spirit of trifling. It were desirable too, as I have had occasion elsewhere to remark concerning your particular friends, that the circle with which you chiefly associate should possess a good degree of intelligence, that thus your social intercourse may be instrumental of improving not only your heart, but your understanding. If you take due precautions on this subject, the time that you pass in society, instead of being lost, may subserve in a high degree, your most important interests; while the neglect of such precautions will render the same hours a mere blank in the period of your probation.

It is natural and proper that those with whom you chiefly mingle should be from the same walks of life with yourself. You may, however, sometimes providentially be thrown among those, the circumstances of whose birth and education have given them a rank quite superior to any which you can claim; and as the case may be, persons of this character may proffer you their confidence and friendship. In all cases of this kind, never suffer yourself to be deluded by any thing that is connected with the pride or circumstance of life; and do not think it a privilege to mingle in society of the most elevated worldly rank, provided there be any thing in it to put in jeopardy your moral principles and feelings. And let me say too, that though you

may very properly accept a fair and honorable introduction into any circle, no matter how elevated, yet
you ought never, by a single action, or word, or look,
to signify a wish for any such distinction. It would
indicate a species of ambition certainly not the most
honorable; and if you should accomplish your object,
it is more than probable that you would meet the
reception which is due only to an intruder.

You would do injustice to yourself, and be wanting
in the discharge of your duty, if you should not occasionally, and even frequently, mingle in the lower
classes of society. Not that I would be an advocate
for confounding or annihilating those distinctions which
Providence has manifestly ordained; nor would I have
you in your intercourse with those in the humble walks
of life, lose sight of the mutual relations which you and
they sustain to each other. But I would have you go
among them with the benign aspect of friendship; and
I would have you make them feel that you recognize
them as fellow-creatures, placed in many respects on
the same level with yourself; and I would have you
leave an impression upon their minds that the adven-
titious distinctions of life are really of little moment
compared with those points in relation to which all
stand upon an equality. The condescending yet dignified familiarity which this species of intercourse would
discover, would do more than you can easily imagine
to render the poor contented and cheerful, and to
secure for yourself their gratitude and confidence.

And let me say too, that its influence upon your own heart would be most salutary—that it would serve to refine and elevate your social affections, and confer dignity on your whole character.

There is one more point involved in the general subject of this letter which is too important to be omitted—I refer to the deportment which it becomes you to maintain towards the other sex. The importance of this, both as it respects yourself and others, you can scarcely estimate too highly. On the one hand, it has much to do in forming your own character; and I need not say that any lack of prudence in this respect, even for a single hour, may expose you to evils which no subsequent caution could enable you effectually to repair. On the other hand, the conduct of every female who is of the least consideration, may be expected to exert an influence on the character of every gentleman with whom she associates; and that influence will be for good or evil, as she exhibits, or fails to exhibit a deportment that becomes her. Indeed, so commanding is this influence, that it is safe to calculate upon the character of any community, from knowing the prevailing standard of female character; and that can scarcely be regarded as an exaggerated maxim, which declares that "women rule the world."

Let me counsel you then never to utter an expression, or do an act that even looks like soliciting any gentleman's attention. Remember that every expression of civility, to be of any value, must be per-

fectly voluntary ; and any wish on your part, whether
directly or indirectly expressed, to make yourself a
favorite, will be certain to awaken the disgust of all
who know it.   I would not recommend to you any
thing like a prudish or affected reserve ; but even this
were not so unfortunate an extreme, as an excessive
forwardness.   While you modestly accept any attentions which propriety warrants, let there be no attempt
at artful insinuation on the one hand, or at taking a
man's heart by storm on the other.

Be not ambitious to be considered a belle.   Indeed
I had rather you would be almost any thing else that
does not involve gross moral obliquity, than this.   It
is the fate of most belles that they become foolishly
vain, think of nothing, and care for nothing beyond
personal display, and not unfrequently sacrifice themselves in a mad bargain, which involves their destinies
for life.   The more of solid and enduring esteem you
enjoy the better ; and you ought to gain whatever of
this you can by honorable means ; but to be admired,
and caressed and flattered, for mere accidental qualities, which involve nothing of intellectual or moral
worth, ought to render any girl who is the subject of
it, an object of pity.   You are at liberty to desire the
good opinion of every gentleman of your acquaintance ;
but it would be worse than folly in you to be ambitious
of a blind admiration.

I will only add, that you ought to be on your guard
against the influence of flattery.   Rely on it, the man

who flatters you, whatever he may profess, is not your friend. It were a much kinder office, and a real mark of friendship, to admonish you tenderly yet honestly, of your faults. If you yield a little to flattery, you have placed yourself on dangerous ground; if you continue to yield, you are not improbably undone.

Adieu for the present.

Your devoted

FATHER.

LETTER XII.

MARRIAGE.

My dear Child—The event of marriage marks an important era in the life of a young female. It introduces her to some new and most interesting relations. It devolves upon her a set of cares and duties and responsibilities, to which she has hitherto been unaccustomed. It usually lays the foundation for increased happiness, or for bitter and enduring and unavailing regrets.

I begin my advice to you on this subject, by suggesting a caution against forming this connection prematurely. There is scarcely any thing that indicates a greater lack of discretion, than for a young girl, at a time when she ought to be giving her thoughts to her books, and thus laying the foundation for respectability and usefulness, to be giving her heart to some admirer, and entering into an arrangement for speedily giving him her hand. The consequence of this is, that she is only imperfectly educated, and not unfrequently is subjected through life, by her deficiencies, to serious inconvenience and mortification. She enters the con-

jugal state miserably qualified to sustain its responsibilities ; and not improbably acquires a cast of character in that relation, which, unfortunately, is too enduring, and which is alike unfavorable to her own
enjoyment, and that of those with whom she is immediately connected.

I advise you, therefore, as you value your prospects
of happiness for life, that you leave all matrimonial
arrangements to a period subsequent to the completion
of your education.   Even if proposals of marriage
should be made to you, and of an eligible kind, previous to that time, it must be an extraordinary case
indeed in which you would be warranted to accept
them.   The very fact of your forming such an engagement, and especially of your suffering it to arrest your
education, would be set down to your disadvantage.
It would be regarded as indicating at least an unfortunate weakness in your character, which would be no
favorable prognostic of a solid and enduring reputation.

Another evil which you should avoid, in connection
with this subject, is that of forming this relation, or
pledging yourself to it, without due deliberation.
Every one knows that there is no department of human
experience which is so fruitful in wonderful occurrences
as this ; and one of the most singular of them all is
the fact, that many a young lady disposes of herself
for life, to a man with whom her acquaintance has
been limited to a few days, or even a few hours.   I
admit that there may be solitary cases of this kind in

which the result is favorable; but no female who makes the rash experiment, has a right to calculate, either from the analogy of experience or the nature of the case, upon any thing else than that the result will be most disastrous. If there be one instance in which there has proved to be a congeniality of thought and feeling favorable to domestic happiness, there are many in which the most opposite tempers and habits have been brought into an unnatural union, and the grave of conjugal happiness has opened beneath the very altar at which the conjugal union was consummated.

I would have you then on your guard against taking a rash step in relation to this important matter. Bear in mind that the decision which you form on this subject is to affect vitally your interests for life; and not only yours, but at least those of one other individual. The consequences of an erroneous decision you will not be able to avoid: they will meet you, and follow you, and attend you through the whole of the rugged path which conducts you to the grave.

Another point of great importance connected with this subject, is the character of the man with whom you are to be united. There are some qualities which may be desirable enough, but are not indispensable: there are others which should be regarded as absolutely requisite, and the opposites of which as absolutely disqualifying for this connection.

It may be a pleasant circumstance, though it certainly ought not to be considered indispensable, that

the individual with whom you are to be connected
should belong to an influential family. This might
secure to you a more valuable circle of acquaintance,
and actually bring within your reach more extended
means, both of improvement and of usefulness, than
you could reasonably expect under different circumstances. It is an important consideration, that in
marriage the wife rises or sinks to the level of the
husband ; and this is a reason why at least a respectable circle of connections on his side, is with her a just
desideratum ; for if there be any blot on the character
of his family which even remotely extends to him, as
soon as her destinies are united with his, she comes in,
almost of course, for her share of the odium ; at least
it has an influence in determining the rank she is to
hold in society.   There are cases, indeed, in which an
extraordinary degree of personal merit completely re-
deems the character of an individual from the deepest
family disgrace, and in such cases a lady would have
nothing to fear from public opinion in giving her hand
in marriage ; but in any other circumstances it were
certainly desirable that she should not throw herself
into a circle of connections of a rank greatly inferior
to those with whom she has been accustomed to mingle.
If Providence should place you by marriage in a more
elevated condition than that to which you have been
accustomed, you may regard it as a favor that demands
your gratitude, and as a means put into your hands for
getting and doing good.   But I repeat, never consider

this indispensable. Be satisfied if the new circle of connections hold a fair and reputable standing.

I regard fortune, as it stands related to the marriage of a young lady, in nearly the same light as family. Great riches are desirable only as a means of doing good: as a means of enjoyment independently of the opportunity they furnish for the exercise of a benevolent spirit, they are really worth very little; and are in no respect to be preferred to a fair competence. If I have any wish that you should be rich, it is not that I may see you in circumstances of splendor, but that I may see you setting a noble example of benevolence—not that you may outshine those around you in the magnificence of your dwelling, or the costliness of your furniture or equipage, but that you may deservedly bear the palm in doing good to the wretched and perishing. But when I remember how often riches become a snare to their possessors, and how many females have been ruined by a sudden elevation to a fortune, I cannot say that I have a wish that you should ever encounter the temptations incident to that condition. It is certainly desirable that there should be a competence on one side or the other, so much as to furnish adequate means, in connection with the avails of some honest and honorable calling, for the support of a family; but within this limit any lady may reasonably circumscribe her wishes.

Do not marry a fop. There is in such a character nothing of true dignity—nothing that commands re-

spect, or insures even a decent standing in the community. There is a mark upon him, an affected elegance of manner, a studied particularity of dress, and
usually a singular inanity of mind, by which he is
known in every circle in which he moves. His very
attitude and gait tell the stranger who he is, though
he only passes him silently in the street. To unite
your destiny with such a man, I hardly need say,
would be to impress the seal of disgrace upon your
character, and the seal of wretchedness upon your
doom.

Do not marry a spendthrift. No, not if he have
ever so extensive a fortune; for no degree of wealth
can secure such a man from the degradation of poverty.
I have in my eye at this moment an accomplished
female—and it were easy to adduce a thousand similar
cases—who married a man of vast wealth, but of prodi-
gal habits; and years have passed away since that
immense fortune has gone to the winds; and the last
remains of it were squandered amidst the tears, and in
spite of the tender and earnest expostulations of a
suffering family. And now if I should look for that
once rejoicing and apparently fortunate bride, I should
go to an obscure cabin of wretchedness, and should
find her laboring with her own hands to provide bread
for her more than orphan children, and she would tell
me a tale of woe which, however familiar to me, would
make me sit down and weep. This same man, who
has plunged her and her little ones into so much

wretchedness, possesses many naturally amiable qualities, and is gifted with enviable powers of mind ; but
unhappily, in early life he became a spendthrift, and on
this rock the fortunes of himself and of his family were
wrecked. If you should ever give yourself to a man
of similar character, you need not be disappointed if
you should experience a similar destiny.

Do not marry a miser. Such a man may be rich,
very rich, but you could expect that his riches would
yield you little else than misery. It is not improbable
that you might have the mortification of being compelled not only to refuse every call of charity, but to
abridge, in a great degree, your own personal com-
forts, and of knowing at the same time that there were
ample means within your reach which yet you were
forbidden to appropriate. If you must marry a miser,
I would say, better marry one who is poor than one
who is rich ; for in the former case, to whatever inconvenience you might be exposed, you would be saved
the disheartening reflection, that you were poor in the
midst of abundance. As I would have you always
cultivate a noble and liberal spirit, I beg you will
never for a moment think of forming a connection
that shall subject you in this respect to the least embarrassment.

Do not marry a man whose age is greatly dispro-
portioned to your own. I will not say that circumstances never exist which justify a deviation from this
rule ; or that there are no cases in which it is violated

that result favorably to the happiness of both parties. But I am constrained to say that such connections present, at least to my own eye, a violation of good taste, and seem contrary to the dictates of nature. Besides, it is an exceedingly awkward thing for a young girl to be going round with a man of triple her own age as a husband, and puzzling all who see them together to decide whether she is the granddaughter or the wife. And a greater evil still is, that there must needs be in many respects an entire lack of congeniality between them. He has the habits and feelings of age, she the vivacity and buoyancy of youth; and it were impossible that this wide difference should not sooner or later be painfully felt. And she may reasonably expect that some of her best days will be spent, not in sustaining the infirmities of an aged father, but in ministering to the necessities of a superannuated husband; and it would not be strange if the burden should be increased by her being compelled to encounter the spirit of complaint and petulance by which old age is often attended. I confess that whenever I see a respectable female in the meridian of life in these circumstances, I regard her with pity; and though I venerate her for the affectionate and faithful attentions which she renders to the man whom she has accepted as her husband, I cannot but wish, for the sake of her own dignity and happiness, that those attentions had devolved upon some other individual.

Do not marry a man who is not industrious in some honorable vocation. It is bad for any individual to be without some set employment: the effect of it is very apt to be, that he abuses his talents, perverts his time to unworthy purposes, and contracts a habit of living to little purpose but that of self-gratification. A man without property, and yet without business, no girl could ever think of marrying, unless she had made up her mind to sell herself to the lowest bidder. A rich man may have retired from active business, after accumulating an estate, and yet may find employment enough in the supervision and management of it ; but if a man has become rich by inheritance, and has never acquired a habit of industry, and has been brought up in abundance to live only as a drone, I would say that it were scarcely more safe to marry him than if he were actually poor ; for this indolent habit is a pledge of the speedy dissipation of his property. A habit of industry once formed is not likely to be ever lost. Place the individual in whatever circumstances you will, and he will not be satisfied unless he can be active. Moreover, it will impart to his character an energy and efficiency, and I may add, dignity, which can hardly fail to render him an object of respect. I should regard your prospects for life as far better, if you should marry a man of very limited property, or even no property at all, with an honest vocation and a habit of industry, than if I were to see you united to one of extensive wealth, who had never been taught to exercise his own powers, and had sunk into the sensual gratification of himself.

Do not marry a man of an irritable, violent, or overbearing temper. There is nothing with which domestic enjoyment is more intimately connected, than a naturally amiable and affectionate disposition; and the absence of this is sure to render a delicate and sensitive female, in no small degree, unhappy. To be compelled to witness frequent ebullitions of angry passion—to hear her well-intended actions often complained of, and her purest motives bitterly impeached— to feel that the stern hand of power is stretched over, rather than the soft arm of kindness laid beneath her— this is a lot from which it would seem the gentleness of female character ought to claim an exemption. I say then, as you value your comfort, venture not to form this connection with a man of an unamiable temper. The only exception to be made from this remark is the case of the man, in whom the principle of religion has gained such an ascendency as to remedy the obliquities of a perverse constitution. But this is one of the highest and holiest triumphs of religion itself; and you ought to gain good evidence that it has accomplished this noble work, before you venture to stake your happiness upon it.

Do not marry a man who is deficient in understanding, or in mental acquisitions. I do not mean that you should look for an intellect of the highest order, or that you should consider yourself entitled to it; but

I mean that a woman of decent intelligence can never be happy with a fool. If you were united to a man of inferior endowments, you would not only lose the advantage which might result from an unreserved intercourse with one of a different character, but you would also be subject to a thousand painful mortifications from the awkward mistakes and ridiculous opinions which would result from his ignorance.   There is scarcely any thing more painful, than to observe a lady and her husband in society when every one feels the superiority of the former to the latter ; and when the wife herself is manifestly so much impressed with his inferiority, that the opening of his lips is the signal for the dropping of her head, or for a blush to diffuse itself over her countenance.   It were certainly a mark of imprudence for any lady to marry a man whom she would be ashamed to introduce into any circle to which she would have access.

Do not marry a man who is sceptical in his principles. If he be an avowed infidel, or if he hold any fundamental error in religion, and yet have every other quality which you could desire, it would be an act of infatuation in you to consent to become his wife.   You cannot, upon any principles of reason, calculate that, if you do this, you will escape injury.   I know an instance in which a young female who had had a religious education married an infidel, a thorough-going disciple of that female monster who has recently gone through this country on the most malignant of all

errands, to corrupt its youth; and the consequence
of this connection has been, that she has plunged with
her husband into the gulf of infidelity, and now openly
reviles the Saviour, and ridicules the most sacred and
awful truths of religion.   I know another instance in
which the husband of a lady of established religious
principles, and of apparently devoted piety, became a
zealous advocate of one of the grossest systems of
error that has ever been baptized into the Christian
name; and though at first she halted, and thought
she could never yield, and even expostulated with her
husband to retreat from the verge of the precipice, yet
she herself at length tremblingly approached, and
finally took the fatal leap; and now, instead of hearing her talk of her reliance on Jesus Christ, and of the
preciousness and the power of his atoning sacrifice,
you will hear her speak of him as only a good moral
teacher, and of her own salvation as if the glory of it
all belonged to herself.   And I doubt not that these
instances furnish a fair illustration of the influence of
such a connection on the female character.   You may
rest assured that you cannot be the constant compan-
ion of an infidel, without breathing an atmosphere
that is strongly impregnated with moral corruption;
and it were little short of a miracle if you should
breathe such an atmosphere, without inhaling the
elements of death.   If I were to see you in these
circumstances, though I would still commend you to
a God of mercy, I could scarcely forbear to weep

over your lot, as if your ruin were actually accomplished.

Do not marry a man of questionable morality. However correct may be his moral and religious opinions, if he be addicted to only a single species of vice, you have no security that he will not sink into the vortex of profligacy. If he be a profane man, he certainly cannot have the fear of God before his eyes, and of course cannot be under the controlling influence of moral obligation. If he suffer himself to be only occasionally found at the gaming table, or if he be addicted in the slightest degree to intemperance, there is a melancholy probability that he will, ere long, become a desperate gambler, and a shameless sot ; and think what it would be to be obliged to recognize such a man as your nearest friend—a man whose character is rendered odious by the very loathsomeness of depravity. I say then, if there be a single exceptionable point in the moral character of the man who offers himself to you, reject his proposals without hesitation; to accept them would in all probability be to prepare for yourself a cup of unmingled bitterness, and possibly to exile yourself from the society of your own friends.

Having said thus much in relation to what should be avoided, and what should be desired, in the character of a husband, I shall close this letter with a few brief directions in respect to your conduct previously and subsequently to your forming an engagement.

If a gentleman addresses you on the subject of mar-

riage, the presumption is that the proposal is unexpected ; and unless you can decide instantly in the
negative, in which case you are bound to apprise him
of your decision without delay, it is proper that you
should make his proposal a subject of immediate and
serious consideration.   In ordinary cases, it is unnecessary to ask the advice of any beside your parents.   It
is due to filial respect that they should be consulted ;
and as they are most deeply interested in your happiness, you could not fail to regard their opinion with
suitable deference.   The two great questions which
you have to decide in order to form your ultimate
conclusion, are, whether, on the whole, you are satisfied with his character, and whether you are susceptible of that degree of affection for him which will justify
this connection.   If, after due consideration, you can
answer both these questions in the affirmative, it may
be safe to decide agreeably to his wishes.   If you are
constrained to answer either in the negative, your duty
to him as well as yourself demands that you should
come to a contrary decision.   And in either case, you
are to lose no time in apprising him of the result.   If
it be that you decline his proposals, make it known to
him in a manner which will be least likely to wound
his sensibility, and let the secret of his having addressed
you never pass your lips.   Your answer in this case
places him in an unpleasant situation at any rate ; and
it were more than cruel to add to his mortification by
giving publicity to the occasion of it.   If, on the other

hand, the result is that you accept his proposals, modestly and affectionately inform him of it, and from that period consider yourself sacredly bound through every vicissitude to become his wife.

An engagement thus deliberately formed, and involving such important interests, it were an indication of something more than weakness to trifle with : it betrays an obliquity of moral feeling, a lack of generous sensibility, and a recklessness of character, which might well lead any gentleman, towards whom the outrage was directed, to congratulate himself upon having been the subject of it, rather than to have had the same qualities to encounter for life, in the nearest and tenderest of all relations. The young lady who wantonly refuses to fulfil an engagement of marriage, in the estimation of all whose good opinion is worth possessing, subjects herself to disgrace ; and you will find, not unfrequently, that Providence ordains something like a retribution in rendering any subsequent connection which may be formed, a source of continual unhappiness.

There are only two cases which occur to me, in which there can be any good ground for a young lady to decline giving her hand in marriage after it has been promised. The one is that in which the person to whom she is pledged, subsequently to an engagement, avows licentious principles, or yields to any immoral practice. The other is that in which she discovers that he has intentionally concealed from her any thing in respect to his character or circumstances, which, had she known it seasonably, would have prevented her forming the engagement. In both these cases it is manifest that she has a right to withdraw ; for in the one, he has voluntarily assumed a character which will be sure to render her wretched, and which, if he had possessed it when the engagement was formed, would have led her unhesitatingly to decline his proposals : in the other, he has gained her consent by deception, and it were impossible that she should be morally bound in a contract, in which the ground on which she would have acted was concealed from her. But where, instead of immorality or infidelity, there has been nothing but misfortune—where the evils which have come upon him, however disastrous, have been the result, not of his own folly or guilt, but of the ordinance of Heaven, there is not the shadow of an apology for her deserting him. I do not say that circumstances may not exist, in which it may be best for both parties that the engagement should not take effect ; but if it is dissolved, let it be a matter of fair understanding, and mutual consent : for her to refuse to fulfil it, were nothing less than a wanton violation of good faith. In becoming engaged to him, she of course consented to share with him the lot which Providence should appoint ; and though she certainly has a right to refuse to share the consequences of vices which he may subsequently have contracted, she has no right to decline a part with him in any afflictions which may be administered by the righteous hand of God.

But you will ask, perhaps, whether there is not yet another case, in which a lady may be justified in declining to fulfil a promise of marriage—that in which she discovers, after she is engaged, that the person to whom she has come under obligation, is not in a sufficient degree the object of her affection. In a case of this kind, I would say, let her beware how she yields to an occasional freak of feeling, or take up the opinion that she has no solid attachment to the individual, because in some particular states of mind she feels or imagines that she feels a sentiment of indifference towards him. But if she is satisfied, after faithfully watching her own feelings, that the prevailing habit of her mind towards him is a habit of indifference or aversion, better perhaps that she should honestly communicate the fact to him ; and no doubt his consent will be readily obtained for the dissolution of the engagement. But in this case, let her remember that she does not rid herself of responsibility. She subjects herself to the imputation of having acted rashly in a case which preëminently required that she should have acted deliberately ; or else of possessing a fickleness of character which must throw an air of suspicion around all her declarations and conduct. The blame of the whole transaction rests upon herself; and the most that she can do is, to transfer it from her conduct at the close, to her conduct at the beginning. Whatever

evil consequences may result to the individual whom
she has disappointed, she must charge, if not upon her
deliberate intention to injure, yet upon her criminal
neglect to avoid it.   Let her never open her lips to
adduce her want of attachment as the shadow of an
apology.   It amounts only to an acknowledgment of
her own caprice, and with the discerning passes for
absolutely nothing.

During the period that intervenes between forming
an engagement and consummating the connection, let
your deportment towards the individual to whom you
have given your affections, be marked by modesty and
dignity, respect and kindness.   Never, on the one
hand, give him the least reason to question the sincerity of your regard, nor on the other, suffer your
intercourse with him to be marked by an undignified
familiarity.   Do all that you can to render him happy ;
and while you will naturally grow in each other's confidence and affection, you may reasonably hope that
you will be helpers of each other's joy in the most
endearing of all human relations.

Ever your devoted

FATHER.

LETTER XIII.

FORMING RELIGIOUS SENTIMENTS.

MY DEAR CHILD—I have now gone through with a consideration of a number of those topics which I deem important to you in practical life.   There is one subject, however, which concerns you more deeply than any other, which remains to be considered.   It is the subject of religion.   It is this which is identified with all your interests as an immortal creature.   A deficiency in other respects may indeed occasion you much inconvenience in the world; but a radical deficiency here must extend its influence beyond the grave, and be felt in the unmitigated pangs of an eternal perdition.

The first branch of this momentous subject to which I wish to call your attention, is the formation of your religious sentiments.   It has been a doctrine unhappily current in modern times, that our religious characters do not, in any important sense, derive their complexion from our religious opinions ; and the practical influence of this doctrine has been exhibited in confounding the

most important distinctions in religion, and in annihilating, in a great measure, the importance of Christian
faith. There are no doubt some truths in religion,
concerning which a mistake does not constitute a
fundamental error; but it is equally true that there
are other great and commanding truths which form
the very soul of piety, the belief of which must enter
radically into our claim to Christian character. For
why have the truths of the Bible been revealed, if it
is not that they should be believed; and of what use
can a revelation be to us, if it be not so explicit that,
with the proper application of our faculties, we can
ascertain what are its leading and essential features?
Moreover, it is the system of divine truth that is the
basis of the whole fabric of practical religion. If religion consist exclusively in being a good neighbor, and
in discharging the duties arising from our social relations, I will admit that faith in its doctrines may be
dispensed with, and yet no very perceptible chasm be
made in the system. But if it be vastly more com-
prehensive in its demands—if it have respect to the
manner of our reconciliation with an offended God—if
it embrace all the mighty machinery of Providence
with respect to our redemption, and all the duties
which we owe to God as well as man, then it were
as absurd to suppose that you can discharge the great
duties of practical religion, while you are indifferent
to the truths of the Bible, as that the man should calculate the distances of the planets, or conduct a ship

through the ocean, who was either ignorant or incredulous in respect to the elementary principles of navigation or astronomy. It is the practical reception of truth that constitutes the very essence of piety; and though there may be a speculative belief of it without a particle of vital godliness, be assured there can be no such thing as genuine practical religion without an intellectual assent to the truth of its doctrines. So far from being unimportant, then, faith is one of the essential elements of piety.

It is then a question of great moment, in what manner you shall become possessed of a correct system of religious opinions. To aid you in this important matter, let me suggest the following brief directions.

Let your opinions be drawn directly from the Bible. I know it is the ordinance of Heaven that the first impressions of divine truth which children receive, should ordinarily be from their parents; and it becomes parents to take heed that those first impressions are correct: but even if your parents should inculcate error, you can no longer be innocent in holding it than while you are incapable of referring their opinions to the law and the testimony. The fact that certain doctrines may have been taught you by the lips of parental tenderness, is certainly a reason why you should not lightly cast them from you; but it is due to your own personal responsibility, that you should receive no doctrines ultimately on mere human authority. So also you may derive much advantage from studying the writings of uninspired men; but you are to bear in mind that they are fallible like yourself, and that in adopting their opinions as your own, without examination, you not only refuse the privilege which God has given you, of thinking for yourself,. but you needlessly run the hazard of embracing error.   While you make whatever use you can of these lesser lights in religion, remember that it is alike your privilege and your duty, to receive the beams of divine truth directly from the Sun of righteousness.   Having satisfied yourself that the Bible is a revelation from God, you are to receive implicitly whatever it contains, however humbling to the pride of the intellect, or opposed to the strongest propensities of the heart.

But you will perhaps ask whether, inasmuch as great minds have arrived at different and opposite conclusions in respect to what the Bible contains, it be not a difficult matter to ascertain its genuine doctrines; so difficult even as to discourage exertion, and furnish some apology for an indolent acquiescence in human authority.   I answer, the fact to which I have adverted may indeed be a reason for not taking up any opinions rashly, but it is also an important argument for not taking them upon trust; for if equally gifted minds have rushed into opposite extremes, it is certain that fine intellectual powers, unless guided by a proper moral influence, do not furnish the shadow of a security against error.   The best interpreter of Scripture, and the only safe one, is good common-sense, under the direction of an humble and teachable temper. Let there be an honest desire to know the truth, and let that desire be directed to the Author of all spiritual illumination, and let it be accompanied with a diligent use of the means which are within our reach, and we need have no fear of being left to any fundamental error. It was the declaration of our Saviour to the Jews, that if they would keep his commandments, they should know his doctrine whether it was of God. If a powerful intellect were essential to the right understanding of Scripture, you perceive at once that to the mass of the world, who possess only common minds, it would be a mere dead letter; but as no higher intellectual powers are necessary than fall to the common lot of man, in connection with that spirit of docility and dependence on divine illumination which all may, if they will, possess, it is manifest that the Bible is fairly open to all; and that every individual is as truly responsible for his religious opinions as for his moral conduct.

In endeavoring to ascertain the doctrines of the Bible, it were desirable that you should bear in mind that the obvious meaning of a passage is generally the correct one; for if it were not so, it would be impossible for mankind in general ever to gain an intelligent conviction of its truths. And if I mistake not, one of the most fruitful sources of error is found in a disposition to overlook the obvious meaning and search for something hidden—something that shall bear the

impression of novelty or of mystery. Far be it from
me to question that the Bible is an inexhaustible
treasury of wisdom ; and it is one of its glorious peculiarities that it will supply materials for reflection to
the noblest intellect, and will reward its most diligent
researches through every period of its existence.
Nevertheless, its leading doctrines are fairly within
the reach of common minds in common circumstances ;
and if you approach it, satisfied to receive the obvious
sense as the true sense, there is no danger that you
will be left to adopt the speculations and vagaries of
a false theology.   A system of error is never deduced
from the Bible easily and naturally ; it is only by being
subjected to the torture of a false construction.

The true system of religion must, in every respect,
correspond with the character of God.   As religion
includes the great system of the divine administration,
it is impossible but that every part of it must be agreeable to his infinitely perfect nature.   Any system of
doctrine, then, which tarnishes any of the divine attributes, which is inconsistent with the highest exercise
of wisdom, goodness, justice, faithfulness, or holiness,
cannot be true, and of course can never have been
revealed by a God of truth.   I admit that in the
manifestation of these perfections, there may be depths
which the line of no human understanding can fathom :
and hence the Bible may and does, in a certain sense,
contain mysteries ; but any doctrine which is perceived
to be irreconcilable with the free and perfect exercise

of any of these attributes, any doctrine which exhibits them at variance with each other, and which would of course leave the divine character to suffer in the view of the intelligent creation, must be the product of proud and erring reason. It will be well for you to inquire in respect to every doctrine that is proposed to your faith, what is its bearing upon the character of God? Is it honorable or dishonorable to any or all of the divine perfections? And if you can decide this question satisfactorily, you need not hesitate as to the ultimate conclusion.

But if the true system of religion must be agreeable to the perfections of God, equally certain is it that it must be accommodated to the condition of man; for one grand design of it is to secure and perfect human happiness. To say nothing of man as a social being, and of the fact that the gospel might be expected to supply rules for the regulation of his conduct in this capacity—it requires but little knowledge of one's self, and little observation of the conduct of others, to arrive at the conclusion that man is a sinner, and as such has exposed himself to the displeasure of God. Most unquestionably, then, no system of religion could be suited to the actual exigencies of human nature, but one that should offer a twofold deliverance—a deliverance from the punishment of sin, and from the dominion of sin; for even if the sinner's guilt were cancelled, yet if he were still left the slave of evil propensities, forgiveness itself would be no blessing. You perceive that a system of religion which should merely prescribe a course of external morality, however it might be accommodated to man as a social being, would be very inadequate to the higher necessities of his condition ; any system short of that which brings peace to the laboring conscience, and sanctification to the polluted soul, in consistency with the honor of the divine character and government, as it could never answer the purpose for which religion was designed, were no better than a mockery of human woe. I need not say that a God of love has never thus trifled with the wants of his creatures.

The true system of religion must also be rational. There may be, and there are, as I have already intimated, doctrines, which in some of their lofty and intricate bearings, we may not be able to comprehend ; but even these doctrines, so far as they are practical in the present state of our existence, commend themselves both to the understanding and the conscience. That they are above human reason certainly cannot be questioned ; but that they are contrary to it never has been, and never can be shown. God addresses us in the Bible as rational beings ; of course the truths which he reveals and requires us to believe, must be conformable to the reason which he has given us, and to which he primarily addresses the revelation. To receive any doctrine that is contrary to reason, were to insult the dignity of our own nature : to reject any doctrine merely because it is above reason, were to claim a right to sit in judgment on the decisions of the Highest.

The true system of religion must be consistent with itself. Truth is always consistent; and as we have a right here to assume that whatever the Bible contains is truth, it follows that there must exist a perfect harmony among its various doctrines. There are indeed some portions of Scripture which may be hard to be understood, and may seem susceptible of some variety of interpretation; but in every such case the true rule is, to judge of what is doubtful by what is clear. And if there be some passages which seem at first view to be inconsistent with the leading doctrines of the gospel, it is right to presume that these constitute an exception from the general remark that the obvious meaning is the true meaning; and in every such case it is probable that a more attentive examination of the passage in its connection will disclose some other sense than that which lies most upon the surface, which is consistent with the general tenor of revealed truth.

The true system of religion must be adapted to make men better. It is impossible but that an infinitely holy God should desire that his intelligent creatures should be holy; and it were absurd to suppose that he should have given them a system of religion which is not adapted to make them so. Accordingly, one grand argument for the divine origin of Christianity is found in the holiness of its doctrines;

in the fact that it exhibits the lines of moral purity in
such boldness and strength that it could have been no
other than a heaven-born system. If this be so, it
follows that no doctrine which is fitted, in any way to
loosen the bands of moral obligation, or to license any
of the evil propensities of the heart, either directly or
indirectly, can be a genuine doctrine of the Bible. It
is safe to presume that that system which fosters a
habit of indifference to practical godliness, and supplies the human heart with arguments for sinful indulgence, is a system of error. It is equally safe to conclude that that system which makes men humble and
meek before God, benevolent and useful to their fellow-
creatures, which exerts an influence, silent indeed, but
certain to bring up the human character towards the
standard of divine perfection, is the system which bears
the signature of heaven, and in the practical reception
of which, men become wise unto salvation.

Before I close this letter, let me urge you, in the
adoption of your religious sentiments, to keep in view
the solemnities of a dying hour. Nothing will be
more likely than this to guard you against fatal error.
If your opinions are formed not only in the season of
health, but with reference to the continuance of health,
and of life, there is great danger that they will prove
to be another gospel, and will be so many thorns in
your dying pillow. There is danger that you will
take up with some wretched system of error ; which will
serve as a present opiate to the conscience, but which

will leave conscience to rise upon you at last, when you can do nothing to silence her accusations. But if in all your inquiries for the truth, you keep in view the last hour of your probation ; and if, before adopting any doctrine or system of doctrine, you ask yourself how you will be likely to regard it when the current of life is ebbing away—whether it will come up to your mind then as a minister of peace or a minister of wrath : I say, if you deal thus honestly with yourself, you can hardly fail to draw from the Bible those precious truths which holy men of God spoke as they were moved by the Holy Ghost.

Commending you to the guidance of God's Spirit, which is able to make you wise unto eternal life

I remain your affectionate

FATHER.

LETTER XIV.

PROPER MODE OF TREATING RELIGIOUS ERROR.

My dear Child—Notwithstanding I have advised you to search the Scriptures as the only infallible standard of religious faith, and to admit no doctrine into your creed merely upon human testimony, you cannot suppose that I am indifferent as to the result of your religious inquiries. I have indeed no fear, if you read the Bible with an honest heart, and with a sincere desire to know the truth, that you will fall into any fundamental or dangerous error: but after all, it must be acknowledged, that not a small number of those who have made the word of God their constant study, and have employed all the power of genius, and all the apparatus of criticism, in their biblical pursuits, have given us the result of their labors in systems of religion which have nothing to sanctify or elevate the affections; nothing to hush the clamors of conscience; nothing to illumine the cheerlessness of affliction, or the desolation of the grave. As the gospel is designed to furnish the means of restoration and salvation to ruined man, I am persuaded, if you examine it with a teachable temper, that you will find its cardinal doctrines to be, atonement by the blood, and sanctification by the Spirit of a divine Saviour. All the other truths which it reveals, you will find to be in perfect consistency with these fundamental ones; making in their combination a system which, while it brings glory to God in the highest, secures to the repenting sinner all, and more than all the blessings which sin has forfeited.

But if the result of your examination should be a conviction that the system to which I have adverted is that which the gospel reveals, you will find that the world abounds with other systems, some of which have scarcely any thing in common with that which you adopt. There is one system which exhibits the gospel as only the religion of nature in a more attractive dress, which pours contempt upon the impressions of the awakened sinner, and blots out the precious doctrine of atonement, and cuts off the only hope of forgiveness, and leaves the mind to wander over a dark, blank waste, collecting as it wanders nothing but impressions of despair. There is another system which perverts the doctrine of redemption, by representing the sacrifice of Christ as cancelling the obligations of holy obedience; substituting for that living faith which purifies the heart and controls the life, the naked impression that Christ died for us in particular. And there is another system still, which completely neutralizes the most awful sanctions of our religion, which represents all its terrors as a fable, and throws wide open the doors of heaven to all the impenitent and unholy. And yet, after all, each of these systems professes to bear the impress of divinity, to be the true and genuine gospel ; and their respective advocates expect you to hail them as fellow-disciples of a common Master. To assist you to a proper decision on this subject, let me request your attention to the following hints.

Make it a rule never to withhold your charity on any slight or equivocal evidence. To declare your conviction that a person holds another gospel, is a thing of too much moment to be hazarded on any grounds which are not the most satisfactory. Better far to err on the extreme of forbearance than of intolerance. Mild measures are much better fitted to exert a reclaiming influence than severe ones. A little severity may place a religious errorist for ever beyond your reach ; whereas, a condescending treatment of him may be the means of dissipating his errors, and establishing him in the truth.

Moreover, I would advise you never to impute to others doctrines which they disavow, because they may appear to you to form an essential part of their general system. Cheerfully give them credit for every truth they will acknowledge ; and be very slow to decide that the connection between a fundamental doctrine and one which is not so, is so close that the latter may not be given up while the former is with some degree of consistency retained. The system of religious truth is indeed perfectly harmonious; but its parts are not all equally important. It is a structure from which you may remove some remote appendage, and you will only injure its proportion, or deface its beauty; but take away one of its main pillars, and the whole fabric tumbles to ruins.

Set it down as a principle, therefore, that all minor differences in religious opinion are to be treated with candor and lenity. It is a reproach to the Christian cause, that the jealousy and intolerance of its professed advocates have erected so many walls of partition to exclude each other from the affectionate interchange of Christian offices; and it is a fact upon which my eye now fastens, as the day-star of millennial glory, that the little strifes and jealousies which have prevailed among different denominations, to the distraction of the church, are beginning to lose themselves in a growing attachment to the common cause. It is our duty indeed to endeavor to reclaim the wandering from every species of error; but the boundary of our Christian charity must be nothing less than that sacred line which encircles the fundamental doctrines of the gospel. If we deliberately exclude from Christian fellowship those who hold the grand peculiarities of our faith, we do it at the peril of rejecting those whom God has accepted.

But while I make all these concessions in favor of catholicism, far be it from me to leave an impression on your mind, that it were safe to receive to the hallowed embrace of Christian charity those who reject any of the fundamental truths of religion. With Christian forbearance in respect to doctrines that are not fundamental, you must combine Christian independence with respect to those that are; and every Christian ought to shrink from any act which implies indifference to the great foundation of the gospel scheme, as he would shrink from the guilt of betraying his Master with a kiss. The only consistent course for those who build their hopes of heaven upon the great truths of the Bible—the only course which their own principles will justify—is to take their stand by the cardinal doctrines of the gospel; and whoever may lift the standard of persecution, or whoever may chant the praises of liberality, to guard these truths with the most sacred vigilance. You may as well think to blend the darkest shades of midnight with the blaze of the noon-day sun, without dissipating the gloom of the one or softening the radiance of the other, as to attempt a compromise between systems of religion, one of which admits and the other rejects the great doctrine of redemption by the atoning blood and life-giving Spirit of Christ.

But notwithstanding you are to be decided in your treatment of fundamental error, you should be on your guard, even in respect to this, against every approach to a bitter and censorious spirit. It is not the spirit which will recommend your religious views to others, or which can furnish to yourself any evidence of their correctness from·their practical tendency. Besides, as I have already intimated, no person was ever reclaimed from error by being insulted or reproached ; but not a few have, by such a course, been steeled against conviction and driven to the extreme of heresy. The person whom you may not be able to recognize as a Christian, you may still treat with the kindness and courtesy of a friend : you may mingle with him in the kind offices and charities of life : you may cautiously avoid reproaching him with his errors : you may go, like an angel of mercy, to his sick-bed ; and you may keep him constantly under the influence of your gentle and winning deportment ; and who knows but that, in this way, you may save a soul from death and hide a multitude of sins?

I will only detain you farther on this subject with one word relative to religious controversy. I am willing you should acquire much theological knowledge, and I will not say that circumstances may never occur, in which it may be proper for you to use it in defence of the truths of the gospel ; but I beg that nothing may ever tempt you needlessly to enlist in any religious dispute. When a woman takes up the weapons of theological warfare, unless at the imperative call of duty, the native loveliness of female character is instantly eclipsed. The modest and retiring virtues, which are the peculiar ornament of your sex, can never find a place amidst the din and clashing of religious combatants. It was my lot, not long since, to encounter a sturdy female polemic in a stage-coach ; and I must confess that, after a little while, she succeeded in driving me effectually from the field—not because I was apprehensive of being crushed by the weight of her arguments, but because, when I came to reflect, it cost me less mortification to yield to her the honor of an apparent triumph, than to keep the attitude which I had incautiously taken of discussing the most momentous of all subjects, in such circumstances, with a talking female, whose element was controversy. I confidently trust that the time will never come when the cause of truth will require the polemic influence of females ; and until that time, I hope you will be contented to leave the business of controversy in other hands.

I have dwelt thus minutely on the several points involved in the subject of this letter, not from a conviction that they would all be of the same importance to you as they might be to a minister of the gospel, but because I wish you, on every subject connected with practical life, to have some fixed principles, which will always be ready for application.

That you may combine that charity which "suffereth long and is kind," with that dignified Christian independence which "holds fast the form of sound words," is the earnest wish of

Your affectionate
FATHER.

LETTER XV.

PRACTICAL RELIGION.

MY DEAR CHILD—In a preceding letter I have endeavored to impress you with the importance of correct views of the great truths of religion. Such views unquestionably lie at the foundation of every right exercise of the affections, and of whatever is truly good in the life. Nevertheless, correct opinions are in themselves of comparatively little importance, unless they are suffered to exert their legitimate influence in forming and elevating the character. You may have "all knowledge and all faith;" you may be unwavering in your conviction of the truth, and even be able to confound gainsayers; and yet, if in all this there be nothing that reaches the heart and influences the conduct, your character in the eye of God is but little removed from that of an unbeliever. You may indeed pass for a Christian with the world, or at least with the undiscerning part of it, and possibly you may imagine yourself one; but the hour of affliction, and the hour of death, and above all, the light of eternity, which will

put your Christianity to the test, will prove it to be a
mere name—an inefficient speculation, not a practical
and sustaining principle.

I have said that practical religion has its beginning
in the understanding. Religious truth being appre-
hended by the mind, spreads its influence over the
affections, and through them that influence is carried
out into every department of action. There is no
mystery in all this, no departure from the common
operation of the principles of human nature; on the
contrary, it is conformed to all the analogies of experience. You believe that a beloved friend is wandering unconsciously on the verge of a precipice, and liable every moment to an irrecoverable and fatal plunge.
This conviction operates irresistibly upon your affections, stirring up in your bosom the deepest compassion
and anxiety. And these same feelings which cause
your heart to throb on account of the danger of your
friend, will lead you to rush towards the fearful precipice, and admonish your friend of her perilous circumstances; and if need be, even to lay hold of her, and
rescue her from destruction. Now this is a fair illustration of what I mean by practical religion. You
read in the Bible, and your own conscience certifies
you of the fact, that you are a sinner; and you read
that God has given his Son to die for your redemption; and that in virtue of that redemption the horrors
of hell may be escaped, and the glories of heaven
attained. These truths you intelligently believe; and

the first effect of this belief is upon the affections—to induce humility, and penitence, and gratitude; and these cannot remain dormant, but must have their operation in the life, in producing obedience to all God's commandments. I ask again, is any thing more simple, more intelligible, more rational than this? And yet this is practical religion—the Christianity, not of the understanding only, but especially of the heart and life.

It is important here to remark, that it belongs to genuine practical religion to control alike the affections and the external conduct. There are those who will have it that to be religious is merely to be susceptible of a warm glow of feeling; to be able to weep profusely under the solemn and affecting truths of the gospel, and to talk with fervor and sensibility of the progress or the decline of religion around them; while the every-day duties of the Christian life, which require action as well as feeling, are unhappily regarded as not among the weightier matters of the law. And there are those, on the other hand, who seem willing to have their hands put in requisition, while yet they practically claim a dispensation for the heart; who cheerfully perform every deed of justice and charity which devolves upon them in their intercourse with their fellow-men, and are even models of external morality, who nevertheless seem to regard repentance and faith and devotion as works of supererogation—at least, as not being essential to the religious character.

Now both these classes are equally in a mistake. Practical religion does not assert its claims exclusively either over the heart or the life, but alike over both. The truths which you believe must exert their influence in the production of holy affections; and those affections must exert their influence in leading to a holy life.   If you make your religion consist merely in feeling, or merely in action, it is at best a partial religion, and will never answer the great purpose of your acceptance with God.

It is a consideration not to be overlooked in connection with this subject, that practical religion never exists independently of the operation of the Holy Spirit.   Such is the natural perverseness of the heart that it never yields up its rebellion, and becomes transformed into the divine likeness, until it is wrought upon by the almighty agency of God.   But this agency, let it always be remembered, is of such a character as not to supersede, but to involve the exercise of the human faculties.   Notwithstanding it is sovereign in its nature, for the very idea of salvation by grace implies sovereignty, it is in perfect accordance with all the laws of moral action; so that the sinner actually makes his very highest efforts precisely at the time when he is the subject of the most powerful divine agency.   The moral actions he performs at the period of his transformation into the divine image, are as truly his own as if he were in every sense an independent agent; and yet God works as really, though not in the same manner, as he did in the original creation. This is the uniform doctrine of Scripture ; and perhaps there is no single passage in which it is more clearly contained, than that in which the apostle exhorts the Christians, to whom he was writing, to work out their own salvation with fear and trembling, giving it as a reason that it was God who worked within them both to will and to do of his good pleasure.

But you will ask, perhaps, whether there is not here something of mystery ; and will inquire for an explanation of this coincidence between the agency of the Creator and the agency of the creature, in the production of this wonderful result. I answer unhesitatingly, that I know nothing on this subject, and expect to know nothing in this world beyond the simple fact. That it *is* so is amply proved, not only by Scripture, but by experience ; but *how* it is so, is a problem which, to say the least, must be reserved to exercise the faculties in a higher state of existence. To reject a fact of which we have all the evidence of which it is susceptible, merely because we cannot explain every thing that is connected with it, were certainly the height of infatuation. Upon this principle we should resign ourselves to a universal scepticism ; for what object is there in nature which, when subjected to a rigid examination, does not present mysteries before which the highest human reason must own itself confounded ?

Practical religion is begun and sustained through

the influence of the truth—the doctrines and precepts
of the Bible. Whether they are contemplated in the
closet or listened to from the pulpit, the Holy Spirit
uses them as the great means of cherishing good affections, and of giving a right direction to the conduct.
The dispensations of Providence also, by being intelligently and seriously contemplated, are rendered subservient to the same end. Whether the heart be
lacerated by affliction, or permitted to rejoice in prosperity, it is the purpose of God, in either case, to add
stability and vigor to the principle of religion. And
if this result be not realized from the means of grace
and the dispensations of Providence, it were in vain
to expect that it should be realized at all.

It is an interesting attribute of practical religion,
that it retains a perfect identity of character in every
variety of circumstances. I do not mean that it con-
founds all the distinctions of society, for such God
never intended should be its effect; but it does, in the
most important sense, lay a foundation for a community of interest and feeling. It conforms the human
character everywhere to the same standard. Everywhere it is accompanied by the same joys and sorrows,
the same fears and hopes and aspirations. You may
bring together persons from the most opposite walks
of society, and if you please from opposite sides of the
globe—persons whose feelings and habits on other
subjects have little or nothing in common, and let each
of them have a principle of genuine religion, and if

they speak the same language they will recognize each other as brethren, and they will be able to report a common experience, and the same spirit of love to Christ, and love to each other, and love to their fellow-men will glow in the bosom of each, and they will be looking forward alike to heaven as their final home. The most cultivated mind, and the most uncultivated, may be brought together, and supposing both to be deeply imbued with genuine religion, they will feel at home in each other's society: there will be one point, though there be only one, at which they can meet on the same level, and hold intelligent and delightful communion.

It is another attribute of practical religion, that it is enduring. Who does not know how fugitive and uncertain are the possessions of the world; how riches take to themselves wings and fly away; how the voice of human applause is often changed, almost in an instant, into the voice of execration; how pleasure turns into pain in the very moment of enjoyment; how even natural affection itself will grow cold and shy, and finally give place to deep-rooted enmity and bitter resentment. But not so with religion. Let the change of external circumstances be what it may, let the fate of other possessions be as it will, this is sure to remain through every vicissitude. A principle of religion, once implanted in the heart, can never be eradicated, and can never cease to exert its influence. It will live in every clime; it will survive every calamity ; and it will brighten into a higher and holier perfection in better worlds.

But not only is practical religion something that will endure, but it is something which, even here, is destined to increase. The principle when first implanted in the heart is indeed feeble in its operations ; and if we were to form our opinion without the aid of experience, and without recourse to the divine testimony, we should decide unhesitatingly that there was little reason to expect that this principle could ever reach a full and strong maturity. But it is the ordinance of God that it should be so ; and the truth is illustrated and confirmed by every Christian's experience. There may indeed be seasons of occasional declension, and there may be seasons of so much darkness as to create the most painful apprehension that the heart has never yet practically recognized the claims of religion ; nevertheless, on the whole, there is a constant progress in the Christian's experience : though his steps may be feeble and faltering, he is still gradually rising towards perfection, gradually gaining new victories over indwelling corruption, enlarging the sphere of his benevolent activity, and coming nearer and nearer the standard of perfect holiness. It is said by an inspired writer, with equal truth and beauty, that "the path of the just is as the shining light, that shineth more and more unto the perfect day."

There are two distinct views in which we may regard practical religion, as it stands connected with the

trials of life : as triumphing over them, and yet as
being advanced and strengthened by them.   When
you talk of human suffering, there is a chord in every
bosom that vibrates in a response to the truth of what
you say.   The trials of mankind are indeed almost
infinitely diversified ; there are scarcely two individuals
whose cup of sorrow is composed of precisely the same
ingredients ; but there is not a solitary individual
whose personal experience does not furnish ample testimony that this world is a vale of tears.   There are
those, it may be,.who to the surrounding world always
bear a cheerful aspect, and who might almost leave
an impression, by the uniform gladness of the countenance, that the sorrows of life had never invaded their
hearts.   But if you could know all that passes within—
if you could, even for a single week, have access to
every secret thought and feeling, you would no doubt
find, that though the countenance seemed always to
beam with joy, yet the heart was often overburdened
with sadness.   There are comparatively few who do
not, at some time or other, become 'the objects of
sympathy from being openly buffeted by the storms of
adversity ; but there are few too who do not experience trials, and sometimes those which bring into the
heart the keenest anguish, of which the world knows
nothing.   Now I say with confidence, that practical
religion confers upon its possessor a glorious triumph
amidst the sorrows of life.   Suppose poverty come
with its train of calamities ; or suppose detraction

point its barbed arrows against a blameless character;
or suppose bereavement cast a withering shade upon
the best earthly hopes and joys; or suppose disease,
which mocks the highest efforts both of friendship and
of skill, impress itself upon the countenance and make
its lodgement in the very seat of life; or suppose, if
you please, that this whole tribe of evils come marching in fearful array to assail an individual at once, I
am sure that I do not say too much for practical religion, when I declare to you that it will enable its
possessor to meet them all in serenity and triumph.
To do this must require a high effort of faith, I acknowledge; but only such an effort as has been exemplified
in the experience of thousands. Oh, when I have
stood amidst· such scenes, and witnessed the sweet
aspirations of hope, and seen the bright beams of joy
irradiate the countenance over which sorrow had
thrown her deepest shades, just as the bow casts its
brilliant hues upon the dark cloud in the going down
of the sun, I have looked upon religion as a bright
angel come down from heaven to exercise a sovereign
influence over human calamity; and if I have formed
a wish or offered a prayer in respect to you at such a
moment, it has been that this good angel may be your
constant attendant through this vale of tears.

But while there is an energy in religion to sustain
the soul amidst the calamities of life, this energy,
instead of being lessened, is increased by the influence
of these calamities. Let religion emerge from a scene

in which she has kept some child of distress from sinking in the deep waters, or in which she has bound up
some heart that has been smitten by the rod of God,
and you shall see her more healthful and vigorous for
having performed these offices of mercy.   In other
words, nothing is so well adapted to purify and brighten
the Christian graces as the furnace of affliction.   And
hence, we look for the noblest specimens of Christian
attainment, not among those who have been always
surrounded with the sunshine of prosperity, but among
those who have had to struggle hard with the calamities of the world.   Not every one, not even every
Christian, whose lot is peculiarly marked by adversity,
experiences, at least in the degree which he might, the
benign effects of which I have spoken ; but the reason
is, that he does not receive his afflictions with a right
spirit : every Christian who is severely tried, may and
ought to be the better for it ; and if he is not so, I do
not say that he may not be saved, but let him take
heed lest it should be so as by fire.

I have spoken of the triumph of religion in affliction,
but she triumphs still more gloriously in death.   Yes,
in that hour, when the clustering symptoms of dissolution proclaim that all is over ; when friends sit down
and weep in silence, because they have done every
thing, and yet the beloved object must die ; when
there is nothing now thought of, either by the dying
or the mourning, but the winding-sheet, and the grave,
and the region that lies beyond it : I say, in that hour,

dark and portentous and terrible as it seems, religion
still triumphs. You may trace her footsteps amid
that scene of desolation in expressions of hope and
peace and joy, and not unfrequently in the serene and
seraphic smile which she has left upon the countenance,
after she has ascended with the spirit to a brighter
world. Infidelity may be brave in life, but she is a
coward in death. True religion is never more cour-
ageous than when she is acting as a guide in the dark
valley—when with one hand she opens the door of the
sepulchre, as a safe though temporary resting-place for
the body, and with the other, the gate of the heavenly
city, as the everlasting residence of the soul.

There is still more to be said for religion, for her
noblest triumph is in eternity. In the religion of the
heart and life, as it exists here, there is the germ of
that exceeding and eternal weight of glory which is
to be the Christian's portion hereafter. Let no one
talk of the brilliancy of an earthly crown, when compared with the immortal splendors of a crown of life.
Let no one value earthly treasures, when compared
with the incorruptible treasures which religion secures
at God's right hand. Let no one set a high estimate
upon the intercourse of earthly friendship, when viewed
in comparison with an everlasting communion with the
spirits of the just made perfect, and with the angels
that burn before the throne, and even with the infinitely
perfect and redeeming God. When we speak of the
joys of heaven, we speak of that, the full extent of

which it hath not entered the heart of man to conceive. It is in that world that religion will sit enthroned, in the majesty of a benign and perpetual triumph.

I have rarely seen the legitimate operations of true religion in forming the character so sublimely exemplified, as in the case of a reverend friend, whom not many years ago I followed to the grave. He was a man upon whom nature had bountifully bestowed her choicest gifts, and who combined every intellectual and moral quality which was necessary to stamp upon his character the seal of greatness. But above all, he was a practical Christian. I knew him when his locks were silvered with years, and his eyes were dim with age, and his limbs tottered beneath their burden. On his furrowed cheek sat the smile of contentment, the living image of peace and joy. He could hardly open his lips but in some expression of penitence for his sins, or of thankfulness for his mercies. While he was cheerful in the enjoyment of temporal blessings, the eye of faith and hope was fixed on heaven. I saw him when the impressions of disease had fastened upon his countenance ; when the symptoms of dissolution were advancing in slow but certain progress, and when eternity was opening its doors to receive his almost disenthralled spirit. I watched him to see if I could discover a symptom of terror or agitation, any thing like the shrinking back of the soul from the grasp of death : but all was calmness and triumph. Just as he had reached the boundary between earth and heaven, I said, "My father, art thou dying in peace?" and his animated expression told me that the songs of seraphs were already trembling on his ear. His dying eye shot forth a beam of rapture, and told in language more than mortal, the vigor of a spirit on the wing for immortality. Never before did I behold Christianity march with so much triumph into the territories of death. The scene is imprinted upon my memory, and I would fain carry the impression of it to the grave.

Your affectionate

FATHER.

LETTER XVI.

SELF-KNOWLEDGE.

My dear Child—I have already endeavored to inculcate upon you the importance of your becoming a proficient in various branches of useful knowledge. There is, however, one branch of which I have hitherto said nothing, which is incomparably more important to you than all human science—I mean the knowledge of yourself. To this deeply interesting subject suffer me now, in a few brief hints, to direct your attention.

In self-knowledge I include, in the first place, a knowledge of your intellectual powers. It implies that you understand the particular bent of your own mind; in which of the faculties, if any, you are especially deficient, and in which of them, if any, you are particularly gifted; whether there is a good degree of harmony naturally pervading the powers of your mind, or whether there is reason for special effort to give to those powers their due balance. It implies also that you understand for what department of mental action your constitution is best adapted, and in what field your efforts will be most likely to be successful.

In the knowledge of which I am speaking there is
also included an acquaintance with your moral dispositions.   There is perhaps as great a variety of
temper among mankind, as of countenance; there
being scarcely two individuals whose natural feelings,
when subjected to a rigid analysis, are not found to
be, in some respects, different.   These original qualities constitute, in a great degree, the germ of the
character; and in most instances, whatever good or
evil is accomplished, whatever happiness or misery is
experienced, no doubt is to be traced, either directly
or indirectly, to the leading tendencies of our nature.
With these tendencies, as it respects yourself, you
should be familiarly acquainted: you should know
what evil dispositions you are most prone to indulge;
at what point you are most susceptible of being successfully assailed by temptation; and at what point
you are capable of encountering temptation with the
best hope of success.

In self-knowledge is further implied a knowledge of
your conduct.   It would seem at first view that every
individual must know this as it respects himself, whether
he desires it or not; but the real fact is, that there is
much in the conduct of most persons, of which, though
it be perfectly open to the world, they contrive to keep
themselves in ignorance.   Not that they are unconscious of their actions as they perform them; but they
suffer them to pass out of remembrance, and never
make them a subject of deliberate review, and still less

do they think of connecting them with each other with a view to ascertain the habit of their life. If you would know yourself, you must be familiar with the tenor of your conduct from day to day—of your conduct in all the circumstances in which you are placed, and in all the relations which you sustain. Whether it be such as conscience approves or condemns, it must not be suffered to escape your observation, or to slide prematurely out of your remembrance.

You must know your motives also—the principles by which your conduct is governed. Not only the general habit of feeling, but the particular motives which prompt to particular actions, should be well understood; for it is possible, that many an action which with the world passes for a splendid deed of benevolence, may, with Him who inspects the motive, be nothing better than an act of gross hypocrisy; and on the other hand, that actions which to the world bear a suspicious character, may, to the Searcher of the heart appear praiseworthy and excellent. In short, every action derives its moral character, not from the external form which it may happen to assume, but from the motive by which it is dictated. If you are ignorant of the motive then, your ignorance is radical. If you do not know this, you probably know less of yourself than those who have an opportunity of inspecting only your external conduct.

It is necessary, further, that you should understand your true character as a sinner before God, though this may be considered as in some sense implied in the knowledge of your external conduct in connection with the motives in which it originates. The knowledge of sin—of one's personal sins—of their extent and aggravation, is obtained only by a practical view of the law of God and of the atonement of Christ; and until this is gained, every other species even of self-knowledge will be to little purpose in the concern of our salvation. This is a point at which, alas, the great mass of mankind are contented to end their inquiries. They are not willing to look far enough to ascertain whether the scriptural doctrine of depravity is true in their own experience, or not; and hence they remain voluntarily and fearfully ignorant both of their guilt and their danger.

You must know, moreover, as a disciple of Christ, what are the sins which most easily beset you; in what way you are most likely to bring a reproach upon the Redeemer's cause; what means you can use with the best effect to increase your spiritual sensibility, your zeal and self-denial and steadfastness in religion. You must know your daily spiritual wants; the various exigencies for which you need God's special grace, and the various channels through which light and hope and joy may be imparted. You must know how to bring home to your heart the precious promises of the gospel, adapting them to different circumstances, and finding in each of them a means of sustaining you in adversity, of quickening you in duty, or of protecting you from the shafts of temptation. You must know the various duties which devolve upon you in the different relations of life—duties which you owe both to God and man ; and the momentous considerations by which these duties are enforced. In a word, whatever relates to your character as an intellectual, moral, or immortal being, you ought distinctly to understand ; and the whole extent of this enters into the true idea of self-knowledge.

The importance of self-knowledge may be evinced by a great variety of considerations. That branch of it which consists in the knowledge of our sins is an essential requisite to our acceptance with God ; for as mankind are saved wholly by grace, they must feel the reasonableness of the terms before they will accept them ; and this they can never do until they are thoroughly convinced of their own depravity. No doubt most of those great errors which sap the foundation of the gospel originate in the want of self-knowledge. Men, from ignorance of their own hearts, and consequent ignorance of their own wants, devise schemes of religion which overlook the necessity of an atonement, or the necessity of a divine influence ; and leave man in the pride of self-confidence to work his own way to heaven, with little or nothing of divine interposition. Hence, we find that whenever any of these refuges of lies are abandoned, the first step in the process is usually a change of views in respect to the human character ; and the same fact takes place previous to every genuine conversion. It is the conviction of guilt and danger that leads to the first efforts to escape from the wrath to come.

But self-knowledge is important, as it is connected not only with the beginning, but with the progress of religion in the heart. It is essential to keeping alive the various Christian graces. It is one of the primary elements of humility; for it is impossible that the Christian should be deeply conversant with his own corruptions, without being abased before God in view of them. It is fitted to cherish a spirit of dependence; for he who knows his own weakness will feel the need of being strengthened from on high; and he who knows the wanderings of his own heart, will regard it a blessed privilege to yield himself up to an all-wise and all-gracious Guide. It has a tendency to bring into exercise a spirit of gratitude; for he who knows himself, knows that it is matchless grace that triumphs over the rebellion of the heart. It serves to awaken and keep alive a spirit of compassion towards those who are indifferent to religion; for he who has seen his own heart in the glass of God's law, and has seen the sentence of his own condemnation staring him in the face, must have a deep sympathy for others still in the same circumstances of jeopardy. And finally, it leads to a spirit of forbearance towards others; a disposition to be charitable in the judgments we form of them; and especially to avoid all needless exposure of their failings; for who that knows his own infirmities and corruptions, can find it in his heart to pass sentence on the character of others, as if he were not himself, in some sense, under the same condemnation?

There is yet another influence which self-knowledge exerts in aiding the growth of the religion of the heart—it secures the Christian, in a great degree, against the power of temptation. He who understands well his own character, who knows what sins most easily beset him, and what temptations are most likely to overcome him, will not needlessly rush into circumstances in which he will be peculiarly exposed to fall; or if he goes into scenes of danger at the unquestionable call of duty, he will go fully apprized of the danger, and girded for a conflict with the enemies which may assail him. The great reason why so many professed disciples of Christ fall into grievous temptation, and make work for bitter repentance, is, that they are deficient in self-knowledge. This was true of Peter, and it has been true of thousands of others, who have made shipwreck of their good resolutions, and have finally been reclaimed by a course of the severest discipline.

Self-knowledge has much to do in promoting the Christian's usefulness. That it must be so, is evident from the remarks already made; for piety is in its very nature active, and prompts to a course of benevolent exertion: hence, if self-knowledge ministers to the growth of piety, it cannot fail to minister to increasing usefulness. It will always be found that just in proportion as the Christian's heart becomes a dwelling-place of good affections, as a spirit of gratitude, of humility, and of dependence on God increases, he will show himself ready to every good word and work.

But it is the tendency of self-knowledge to promote the Christian's usefulness still further, as it assists him to select a proper field for his activity. If an individual happens to get into a sphere for which he is particularly disqualified, let his intentions be as good as they may, and let his activity be ever so great, it is not improbable that greater injury than benefit will result from his exertions; whereas the same amount of effort, in a field for which Providence had fitted him, might exert a blessed influence on many successive generations. Self-knowledge is the grand security against mistaking in this matter. If you know well the peculiarities of your own mind and temperament, the weak as well as the strong points in your character, you will be in little danger of engaging in enterprises for which God never designed you; and on the other hand, you will be likely to employ your powers on the most suitable objects, and with the best effect.

Self-knowledge is fitted, moreover, to promote the Christian's usefulness, as it imparts to him stability of character. If you know little of yourself, you will almost of course be liable to a sudden adoption of opinions respecting truth and duty, and to an equally sudden abandonment of them; and this will produce a habit of instability both of feeling and action, which will injure your usefulness by weakening the confidence of others in your judgment, and by rendering your efforts feeble and inefficient.   On the other hand, an intimate acquaintance with your own heart, as it will keep you from engaging in rash enterprises, will also make you resolute and stable in respect to those in which you actually engage; and your facilities for doing good will be increased by the favorable regard which this habit of stability will secure to you from the surrounding community.   Is it not manifest, then, that self-knowledge is one of the best pledges for well-directed activity and usefulness?

But how is this most desirable attainment to be made?   It is within the reach of every individual, and yet there is reason to fear that the multitude remain strangers to it.   The reason is, that they shrink from the effort necessary for knowing themselves on the one hand, and dread the result of an examination on the other.

If you would know yourself, it is essential that you should habitually and faithfully perform the duty of self-communion.   You must not be contented with looking merely at the external act, but faithfully investigate the motives and principles of your conduct. You must compare your actions, not with any human standard, but with the rule of duty which God has revealed in his word.   You must let your examination be conducted with great vigilance, with due delibera-

tion, with unyielding resolution, and with entire impartiality. You must examine the operations of your
mind and heart in different states of feeling, and in
every variety of circumstances; and must compare
the result at one time with the result at another; that
thus you may be able to ascertain the general tenor
of your thoughts and feelings. A superficial and occasional inspection of your heart will contribute little
to your stock of self-knowledge, and may even expose
you to fatal self-deception; but an examination, conducted in the manner which I have described, cannot
fail in the end to render you intimately acquainted
with yourself.

Judicious and free conversation with Christian friends
is another important means of acquiring self-knowledge.
The truth is, that we often by our conduct exhibit feelings and traits of character which we are not conscious
of possessing; and thus put it in the power of our
friends to reveal to us the secrets of our own hearts.
And though this is a matter upon which we ought not
to converse too indiscriminately, yet it may very safely
and properly become a subject of conversation with
those in whom we repose special confidence; and they
may be of immense advantage to us by giving us their
honest impressions in respect to that part of our conduct which falls under their observation. Nay, we
may often learn important lessons in respect to ourselves by watching the conduct of others towards us;
for it is more than probable, if they know us intimately,

that they judge correctly respecting our character, and their treatment of us will almost certainly reveal their true opinion. If, for instance, the careless world treat a professing Christian habitually as if he were one of themselves, you may calculate, with absolute assurance, that he has become a backslider: and many a professor, no doubt, if he would, might learn from the treatment which he receives from the world, that he is beginning to wander, while he has scarcely begun to suspect it from observation upon his own conduct, or from an examination of his own heart.

Reading the Scriptures and prayer are among the most important of all the means of self-knowledge. The former, by exhibiting in the divine law a perfect standard of duty, and by exhibiting the character of man in every variety of condition and under every kind of influence, brings us acquainted, more than all other books, with the most secret springs of human action. The latter secures God's blessing upon every other effort, while it brings to our aid a direct divine illumination. Study the Bible then daily and diligently, and pray without ceasing for the enlightening influence of God's Spirit, and you will soon be a proficient in self-knowledge.

Your affectionate

FATHER.

LETTER XVII

SELF-GOVERNMENT

My DEAR CHILD—Perhaps there is nothing in which religion displays a more heavenly triumph than in the power which she gives us of controlling ourselves. The shock of the apostasy has given to the moral principles of our nature a wrong direction; and all the power which reason and conscience can exert, without the influence of religion, is insufficient to subdue and control our native propensities. Practical Christianity, however, is powerful enough to deliver us from this unhappy thraldom. It is by her omnipotent and all-pervading influence that the thoughts are disciplined to flow in a proper channel, the passions and appetites subjected to the control of reason, and the tongue bridled against sinful levity and unhallowed reproach.

But inasmuch as religion regards you as a rational and accountable being, she accomplishes this redemption not by any magical or arbitrary process, but by subjecting you to laws which are altogether fitted to your moral nature. If then you will escape from the dominion of unhallowed thoughts and tempers, you must surrender yourself to the practical influence of the gospel, you must resolutely break away from the enchanted ground of temptation; you must be daily conversant with that almighty power which alone can arm you for a conflict with yourself; you must learn to detect the deceitful and wandering imagination, and station a vigilant sentinel at every watchtower of your heart. To think of acquiring a habit of self-government independently of the influence of religion, were as wild as to think of assuaging the elements by a word, when they are wrought up to the fury of a tempest.

An important part of self-government respects the thoughts. It is a delusion into which we easily fall, that if our external deportment is correct and exemplary, it matters little what are the secret operations of the mind. The thoughts, because they are invisible, are regarded as being scarcely within our control; and no doubt many a mind finds an apology for gross and habitual wanderings, in a sort of indefinite conviction that the imagination was made to have its own way, and therefore it is in vain to attempt to restrain it. So long as the tongue is kept from giving utterance to the evil thoughts which occupy the mind, it is most unwarrantably concluded that they may be indulged without injury. But the thoughts, let it be remembered, are among the primary elements of moral action. If they are habitually wrong, the feelings will be so also; and the thoughts and feelings together

constitute, in the view of God, the whole moral character. The moment you yield to the conviction that no
restraint is needed here, you resolve on a course which
must make you odious in the sight of Heaven; and
nothing but the well sustained and undetected character of a hypocrite can save you from being odious in
the view of the world.

I acknowledge that the duty to which I am urging
you, that of exercising a suitable control over your
thoughts, is one of the most difficult to which you can
be called; and it were in vain to think of discharging
it without severe effort. You should endeavor habitually to realize that you are as truly responsible to God
for the indulgence of a vain imagination, as you would
be if every evil thought that rises in your heart were
embodied in the form of a palpable action. You
should guard against the beginning of such a habit;
for if it were once firmly established, there is scarcely
any other habit which might not with less difficulty
be broken up; for this reason especially, that this is
invisible, and of course not to be affected by any considerations drawn from external circumstances. You
should guard against all those scenes and occasions
which may be likely to throw you into the power of
these invisible tyrants, or to lead you, even in the
smallest degree, to relax your circumspection. You
should especially guard the senses; for these are the
principal avenues through which vain thoughts find
their way into the soul. But let the effort necessary

to this branch of self-government be as severe as it may, let nothing tempt you to neglect it; for you may rest assured that it constitutes, in an important sense, the keystone to a virtuous character.

But you must not only look well to the government of the thoughts, but also of the passions and affections. This especially is the department of the soul in which motives operate, and where are fixed all the springs of human accountableness. It is indeed at the torch of the imagination that the passions are usually kindled; and this is a reason why the imagination should be kept with all diligence; but the passions will never be held in subjection, unless there be employed in reference to this object a great amount of direct effort. So active and powerful are they that they will often plead their own cause, not only eloquently but successfully, against reason, conscience, and character; and many an individual has sacrificed at the shrine of passion, every thing dear on earth, every thing glorious in eternity.

As there is a great variety in the human constitution, the different passions will be found to exist in different individuals, with very unequal degrees of strength; insomuch that what constitutes the ruling passion of one, may operate with comparatively little strength in another. It becomes therefore a matter of no small moment to each individual to apply the most active restraint where it is most demanded; not indeed to be negligent in respect to any of the passions, but to be specially armed for a conflict with those which are the most formidable.

Guard against the improper indulgence of anger. The evil of giving way to hasty and violent resent ments is always great, and sometimes irretrievable. You thereby deprive yourself for the time of the power of regulating your own conduct, while yet you must be responsible for all its consequences; for neither common-sense nor conscience, the law of God nor the law of man, excuses a bad action because it has been performed in a paroxysm of passion. You may, by a single word spoken at such a moment, leave a sting in the heart of a friend which no acts of subsequent kindness may be able fully to extract; a friend too, it may be, for whom, in an hour of reflection, you would have done or suffered any thing. Or you may need-lessly subject yourself to the ridicule and sneers of those who are below you; of those who are upon the look-out for your foibles, and stand ready to make the most of them. Nay, you may bring yourself into sad disrepute with all around you, and may greatly cloud your worldly prospects, and prepare for yourself a scene of mortification and disgrace which will last while you live, and then be entailed upon your memory. In short, if you exercise little or no self-control in this respect, you can have no security for your comfort—no security for your character.

If I were to prescribe one of the best remedies for a hasty spirit, I should say, accustom yourself to be silent under provocation. It is a maxim with some, that the best way of encountering insult is to speak out whatever is in the heart, and thus let an angry spirit exhaust itself in a torrent of reproach. Precisely the opposite of this is the course which I would recommend. If you begin to talk while you are in a passion, the effect will almost certainly be that your feelings will become more and more excited; for while there is a tendency to such a result, in the very act of uttering your feelings you will be in danger of saying things which will bring back upon you still heavier provocation. If, on the contrary, when you feel the first risings of resentment, you make it a rule to pause and reflect on the evil consequences of such a spirit, and on the guilt as well as the folly of indulging it, you will probably have occasion to pause but a moment before reason will resume her dominion, and you can converse with composure and dignity. And it is worthy of remark, that while such a course will exert the happiest influence upon yourself, it will, more than any thing else, disarm others of a spirit of provocation, and thus secure you from insults and injuries. Mark it as often as you will, and you will find that the individual who is most calm and patient in the reception of injuries, is the very one who has the fewest injuries to endure.

In connection with a spirit of anger, I may mention a kindred passion, that of revenge; for experience proves that revenge sometimes deforms and blackens

even the female character. Anger is most commonly
the exercise of a rash and hasty spirit; and it often
happens, that though it may be followed by the most
lasting evils, yet it passes away in an hour, or even in
a moment. Revenge is more thoughtful, more deliberate ; its purposes are indeed usually conceived in anger,
but often executed with coolness, and sometimes even
in the dark. Whatever injuries you may receive,
never allow yourself for a moment to meditate a purpose of retaliation. You are not indeed required
tamely to surrender your rights to every one who may
choose wantonly to invade them, for that would be
little less than to court injuries ; but you are never,
under any circumstances of provocation, to depart from
the golden rule—never to form a design, or even to
harbor a wish to return evil for evil. Nothing is more
noble than to be able to forgive an injury, instead of
inflicting injury again. You remember that most
beautiful and touching instance in which the Saviour,
in the action of death, commended to the forgiveness
of his Father his enemies and murderers. Who ever
contemplated this incident in his life, without a deep
impression of reverence and moral sublimity? Who
ever doubted that the imitation of such an example
would confer true dignity of character?

There is envy too—one of the meanest of all the
passions, and yet it too often gets a strong lodgement
in the breast. You mistake if you imagine that this
is confined chiefly to persons in the lower walks of

life ; it is, for aught I know, just as common among
the more elevated as the more obscure ; and there is
nothing in external circumstances that can prevent its
operation. It is alike offensive in the sight of God and
of man. If the object towards which it is exercised be
wealth, or splendor, or any thing connected with the
pride and circumstance of life, it is unreasonable, because nothing of all this is essential to human happiness ;
and if God in his providence places these temporal
possessions beyond our reach, we ought to conclude
that it is best that they should be withheld from us.
If the object be intellectual strength or culture, this
passion is unreasonable still ; for it implies either a
dissatisfaction with the powers and opportunities which
God has given us, or else an unwillingness to use the
exertion necessary for making the best of them. And
even if the object be moral excellence, the unreasona-
bleness of indulging this feeling is not at all diminished ;
for whatever is elevated in moral or Christian character, every individual is commanded to attain ; and to
each one God is ready to give the necessary helps for
doing so. And it is not only an unreasonable, but a
malignant spirit. It looks with an eye of hatred upon
a brother, for no other reason than because he is, or
is supposed to be, a special favorite of Providence.
If this hateful passion ever rises in your breast, banish
it as one of the worst enemies of your happiness, your
character, and your soul. Or, I would rather say,
cultivate such a habit of feeling as shall be an effectual

security against it. Think how many reasons there
are why you should delight in the happiness of your
fellow-creatures ; and let those considerations operate
not only to keep you from being envious, but to make
you grateful, when those around you are in any way
the special objects of the divine goodness.

The various appetites which have their seat in the
animal nature, ought also to be kept in rigid subjection.
These appetites were given us for important purposes ;
but who does not know that in a multitude of instances,
instead of accomplishing the end for which they were
designed, they actually become the ministers of death?
Many, even of your own sex, and those too, the circumstances of whose birth and education might have been
expected most effectually to shield them from such a
calamity, have resigned themselves to a habit of intemperance, and have ultimately sunk to the lowest
point of degradation. Once they would have been
startled with horror by the thought of their present
condition ; but the almost imperceptible indulgence
with which they began, gradually increased till they
plunged into gross dissipation, and exiled themselves
not only from decent society, but from the affections
of their own kindred. What young female can contemplate examples like these, and quietly repose in the
conviction that she is beyond the reach of danger?

I must not omit to speak here of the government of
the tongue, though much of what appropriately belongs to this branch of the subject has been anticipated

in a preceding letter. If your thoughts and passions and appetites are kept in due subjection, the proper regulation of the tongue will be a matter of course; for "out of the abundance of the heart the mouth speaketh." There is the deceitful tongue, which deals in misrepresentation and falsehood. There is the loquacious tongue, that monopolizes the conversation of every circle, and tires by its perpetual garrulity. There is the vulgar tongue, that throws out indecent allusions, and finds its element in grovelling subjects. There is the inflamed tongue, that busies itself in the propagation of scandal, and loves to array friends against each other, and keep neighborhoods in commotion; and there is the flattering tongue, which would pour into your ears the sweetest strains of applause, and would make you think that you are too good for this world, and are as lovely and beautiful as an angel. Take heed that *your* tongue is never prostituted to any of these unworthy purposes. And recollect that while the thoughts and passions and appetites control the movements of the tongue, the tongue in its turn exerts an influence upon *them* either for good or evil. If you cherish an habitual impression of the presence of God, and in all that you say endeavor to keep yourself subject to the dictates of an enlightened and wakeful conscience, your tongue will indeed be the glory of your frame, and a source of blessing to yourself and others; but if not, take heed lest it should prove a world of iniquity, and should be the instrument of bringing upon you a fearfully aggravated condemnation.

In respect to the importance of self-government, I surely need not enlarge. You cannot fail to perceive that it is essential to all true dignity of character, and to all that enjoyment which is worthy of your rational and immortal nature. Without it you may imagine yourself free, but you are really in the most degrading vassalage. Without it, you may consider yourself respectable, but all virtuous beings will regard your character with pity and abhorrence. With it, you will rise up to the true dignity of a rational being, and act in consistency with your immortal hopes.

Your ever affectionate

FATHER.

LETTER XVIII.

HUMILITY.

My DEAR CHILD—It is one of the most distinguishing and lovely features of Christianity, that it not only inculcates, but actually produces and cherishes the grace of humility. So remote is this from the spirit of paganism, even in its least exceptionable forms, that the language of the nation more enlightened than any other at the time of the advent of Christ, did not supply a word expressive of what we mean by humility. It belongs to the gospel to have made the discovery that there is a species of self-abasement which, while it is befitting our character as sinners, is intimately connected with the highest moral dignity.

There is, however, much that passes more or less current in the world for humility, which does not deserve the name; and in respect to this, as of all the other graces of the Christian, it is important that you should be able to detect its counterfeits. There is, for instance, an abject spirit, which is grovelling in its nature, and finds its appropriate element amidst a corresponding set of objects; whereas true humility lifts the soul from the dust and brings it in contact with some of the most glorious objects in the universe.

There is also a desponding spirit, which lives upon doubts and anxieties in respect to personal religious experience, and turns away from the promises as if they were made only for those who could appropriate them with absolute assurance : this cannot be genuine humility, for it is the legitimate offspring of unbelief, and humility is always connected with living faith. There is, moreover, a timid spirit, which attempts little, and therefore accomplishes little ; on the ground perhaps that there may be danger of overrating one's own powers ; but humility is perfectly consistent with forming large plans, and entering upon the most extensive field of action, provided it be from Christian motives. It is a mistake into which many persons fall, that pride is always the accompaniment of rank, and that humility is found almost of course among the lower classes. There may be more, I acknowledge, in the one case than the other, to foster a spirit of pride ; though even in this respect, on account of the different standards that exist among various classes, there may be less difference than might be imagined ; but the truth undoubtedly is, that you may be very humble in any station to which Providence can raise you ; or you may be very proud in the obscurest situation to which you can be reduced.

But there is nothing in which a spirit of false humility discovers itself more decisively than in speaking more unfavorably of one's self than facts will warrant. Expressions of this kind almost uniformly fail of their

object; for it requires but little discernment to detect
the unworthy motive. If you attribute to yourself
faults with which you and the world know that you
are not chargeable, instead of being taken as a mark
of humility, it will be regarded as an indication of a
weak mind, and an unworthy attempt to provoke commendation which you do not deserve.

One of the most common, and to me one of the most
painful exhibitions of this spirit, consists in the indis-
criminate and often somewhat public confessions of
professed Christians in respect to their own coldness
and neglect of duty, when they manifest no disposition
to be more active and faithful. All this kind of self-
righteous gossiping, for I can call it nothing better, is
often found a most convenient substitute for doing
one's duty; and, if I mistake not, many a lukewarm
Christian has found in these unmeaning confessions an
opiate to his conscience, in the strength of which he
has gone many days. And I am constrained to express my conviction that this same spirit not unfrequently operates in prayer; and that acknowledgments
of grievous backsliding are attempted to be poured
into the ear of mercy, which are really very little felt,
and which are scarcely designed to answer any other
purpose, I almost shudder to say it, than to lessen the
remorse which attends a habit of sinning. Wherever
you see active efforts to forsake sin and to rise to a
higher tone of religious feeling and action, there you
make take it for granted is true humility: but where

nothing appears but confessions of delinquency, however deep or often repeated, you may rely on it, the
genuine grace is not there.

True Christian humility is one of the effects of divine
grace operating upon the heart.   The apostle has beau-
tifully described it in few words, as a disposition which
leads us not to think more highly of ourselves than we
ought to think.   It discovers itself in heartfelt expressions of abasement before God, and in the modesty of our
appearance, conversation, and pursuits before the world.

It is one of the first exercises of true humility, that
it leads to the renunciation of our own works as a
ground of justification.   Notwithstanding the Christian may be conscious of being enabled really to exercise some graces, yet when he compares his character
with the standard, he finds such an awful deficiency
that he dares not trust to his own doings for a moment.
When he asks himself whether he is really sincere,
whether he loves God, and is seeking to advance his
glory, his conscience returns an affirmative, though
perhaps a somewhat trembling answer.   But when he
inquires whether his offences do not fearfully prepon-
derate, much more whether he has a right to hope for
salvation on the ground of his own obedience, his mind
is instantly directed to the righteousness of Christ.
Sometimes, it may be, when the candle of the Lord
shines bright upon him, he is ready for a moment to
imagine that his mountain stands strong ; but not improbably the change is so sudden to a state of dark-

ness and doubt, that he begins to question the reality of his whole experience. Whoever has yet to learn that his own strength is weakness, and that his own righteousness is nothing in the affair of justification, has not entered upon the Christian life, and is of course a stranger to genuine humility.

Closely connected with the renunciation of our own works, is hatred of sin. It is true indeed that the Christian does not contemplate sin in all its malignity: he does not realize how deep is the depravity which reigns in his own heart; nor are the views which he has of the subject equally clear at all times: still, he has had such views at some period or other as to bring him into the dust before God. And this self-abasement does not arise from the contemplation of sin as it is acted out in its more odious forms in the world, so much as from a view of his own personal depravity. It is the principle of sin, especially as it operates in his own bosom, which awakens his most cordial hatred, and enlists his most active opposition.

The motives for the cultivation of humility are so numerous that I can only glance at a few of them. One of them is to be found in the fact that this grace is an essential and prominent part of Christian character; and that you have so much and only so much of true religion as you have of true humility. One of the fathers said, "If I were asked what is the first grace of the Christian, I would say, humility. If I were asked what is the second, I would say, humility. If I were asked what is the third, I would still say, humility for ever." No doubt pride, in some form or other, is a ruling principle of the corrupt heart: if then you would reach a high point in sanctification, guard against pride in all its forms, and be always clothed with the garments of humility.

And if this be so important a part of Christian character, I hardly need say that it is essential to the Christian's comfort. Every thing in the universe is part of a system ; and when it is in the place appointed for it, it is either at rest or in harmonious motion. This is true of ourselves: but pride disturbs this harmony, and by removing the soul out of its proper sphere, makes it restless and unhappy. The great secret of true happiness in any station is to have a principle introduced, and in exercise, which will restore harmony to the passions, and will relieve us from the conflicts and tumults they occasion.

Not a small part of the unhappiness that exists in the world, results immediately from the operation of pride. Where in the annals of woe will you find characters that have been subjected to deeper suffering than Pharaoh and Nebuchadnezzar and Herod? But in each of them pride was emphatically the ruling passion, and to it they sacrificed every thing valuable in time and eternity. And a similar result we have seen in many cases that have fallen under our own observation : persons who have gloried in their fancied superiority to those around them—a superiority perhaps which has been conferred by the glitter of wealth or the breath of applause, have at length been permitted to fall, not only into entire insignificance, but into the deepest degradation ; thus verifying the divine declaration, that "he that exalteth himself shall be abased." On the other hand, wherever the genuine humility of the gospel appears, whatever the external circumstances may be, there you may look with confidence for true happiness. Even under the darkest cloud of adversity humility diffuses a sweet peace, and sometimes an unutterable joy through the soul. Who has not seen the humble Christian breathing out his life in triumph? Who has not seen the proud worldling dying without consolation and without hope?

Let me say too that a spirit of humility will go far towards rendering you acceptable and useful in your intercourse with the world. The conduct in which a proud spirit discovers itself, is almost sure to revolt even the proud themselves, when they witness it in others ; and as for the humble, they cannot fail to regard it as an odious quality, though they may pity those who are the subjects of it. The usefulness of the proud man must be limited, not only because his pride will probably keep him within a narrow sphere, but because the efforts which he actually makes, being prompted by a wrong spirit, will not be likely to draw down upon them the blessing of God. It were worth while to be humble, if it were only for the advantages which humility secures in the present life.

Remember that a proud spirit cannot be concealed. If it exists in the heart, all the means you can use to conceal it from the world will be in vain. It will discover itself in your conversation and deportment, and will give a complexion to your whole character. I have known instances in which the manners of persons have been formed in the morning of life under the influence of a principle of pride; and though they afterwards gave evidence of true piety, the haughty and overbearing manner which they had early acquired, in spite of all their exertions to the contrary, continued to the close of life. Wherever this spirit is acted out in the manners, it is always odious; but where it appears in the manners of a female, it receives, from the world at least, a double condemnation.

With a view to increase a spirit of humility, meditate much on the character of God, and especially his holiness, as it is exhibited in the work of redemption. Meditate much on the example of Christ, who humbled himself and became obedient to death, even the death of the cross. Endeavor to gain deep impressions of your guilt, and of the punishment to which your sins have justly made you liable. Dwell upon the goodness of God, as it is manifested to you in your unnumbered mercies; on the promises of God to the humble and contrite; and remember that one employment of the redeemed in glory is to cast their crowns at their Saviour's feet. Your affectionate

FATHER.

LETTER XIX.

DEVOTION.

My dear Child—You cannot be ignorant that one of the primary elements of Christian character is a spirit of devotion. There is indeed much that assumes the name of devotion, which has nothing in common with genuine piety, while yet it is adopted as a substitute for it. There is the habit of entire seclusion from the world ; there is the practice of severe self-mortification—doing penance to atone for one's misdeeds, which has been and still is, to a considerable extent, current in the world, under the name of devotion ; though I need not stop to show that all this is merely the operation of a spirit of self-righteousness, and in many instances no doubt of deliberate hypocrisy. It makes nothing against true devotion that it has its counterfeits, and that some of them are very fair, while yet they are very base. It is not always easy at first view to distinguish the genuine from the counterfeit coin, though when each comes to be subjected to a rigid analysis, they are found to have nothing in common but the external appearance. In like manner, there often seems a close resemblance between true and false devotion ; and it may not always be possible for the undiscerning eye of man to discriminate between them ; but to the eye of Omniscience, they are as widely different from each other as the most opposite elements.

True devotion is that spiritual intercourse which the soul has with its Maker and Redeemer ; it is the intelligent communing of man with the almighty Spirit, in acts of grateful and reverential homage. The intellect rises up to a contemplation of God—of his character and of his works—and the affections rise along with it, and the whole soul is awed and melted and quickened by coming in contact as it were with the infinite Majesty. The primary elements of devotion are the truths of God's word. Without an intelligent view of these truths, there may indeed be a warm glow of feeling, but it is not kindled by the breathing of God's Holy Spirit, and is nothing better than a gust of enthusiasm. The person who is in the exercise of a truly devotional spirit, even amidst its deepest fervors, can assign a good reason for every emotion that he experiences ; he can point to some doctrine or some promise in God's holy word to justify all that he expresses, and all that he feels. Devotion, just in proportion as it subsists upon any other aliment than the simple truth, becomes blind, and of course spurious.

The spirit of devotion finds its element peculiarly, though by no means exclusively, in the closet. If it were compelled to encounter continually the cold atmosphere of the world, it would seem scarcely possible but that it should languish and finally expire ; but it goes back at short intervals to the closet, and then comes forth invigorated by its secret communings with the fountain of light and strength. It is of great importance that the duty of secret prayer should be performed not only frequently, but at stated seasons ; for while it is most intimately connected with the maintenance of a spirit of devotion, and of course with growth in grace, a habit of irregularity is almost sure to beget a habit of coldness ; and by this very process many a Christian has passed in a short period from a state of high religious enjoyment and activity to a state of grievous backsliding. Indeed, I think there are few cases of religious declension which will not be found to have originated in a neglect of the closet. And on the other hand, where these duties are intelligently, devoutly, and regularly performed, you may look with confidence for a vigorous tone of religious feeling, and a consistent course of religious action.

But as we are social beings, it is right that devotion should sometimes be a social exercise ; and hence we find that God has instituted the ordinance of public worship. Where Christians come together in the great congregation, and there is the union of many hearts, the flame of devotion sometimes burns with peculiar ardor, and the communion of saints furnishes some feeble impression of what their communion will be when they shall unite in the songs of heaven, and cast their crowns together before the throne. As you value the pleasure and the privilege of devotion, and as you regard the will and authority of God, you will make it a point never, from any insufficient reason, to be absent from his house. I say nothing here of the preaching of the gospel, though this too is an ordinance of divine appointment, and one of the most important means of improvement in piety; but I speak now of public worship in distinction from the dispensation of the word; and of that I affirm unhesitatingly, that you cannot neglect it, or engage in it with a divided heart, without bringing spiritual barrenness and death into your soul.

In addition to the public devotions of God's house, in which you should always mingle, unless providentially prevented, I would earnestly recommend the practice of meeting occasionally a few female friends for the purpose of social prayer. The practice which has prevailed in some places, of females conducting the devotions of a public meeting in which the sexes are indiscriminately mingled, seems to me as contrary to Scripture as it is revolting to a sense of propriety; and though I acknowledge there may be cases in which a pious female may be justified in offering a prayer in the presence of one or more of the other sex, yet I am constrained to regard these cases as exceptions from a general rule, and as of rather unfrequent occurrence. But that females should meet for social prayer, and

especially in a small circle—females too who are in
the habits of intimacy, is not only perfectly consistent
with the most rigid propriety, but is due to the relation which they sustain to each other as fellow-disciples of the Lord Jesus. While such a habit is fitted
to strengthen their Christian friendship, and increase
their interest in each other's spiritual welfare, it furnishes rich materials for pious reflection, and renders
their intercourse fruitful in blessings to themselves, and
it may be hoped to others also. If any degree of
prejudice has existed in any part of the Christian community against meetings of this description, it is manifestly in a great measure removed ; and it is an auspi-
cious circumstance that Christian females, in the higher
as well as humbler walks of life, have associated so
extensively in smaller or larger circles with reference
to this object.

There are some things which operate as hinderances
to devotion, against which you ought to guard with
unremitted vigilance. There is a habit of sloth, which
will inevitably keep the soul from rising to God, and
will render every spiritual perception indistinct, and
every spiritual exercise feeble. There is ignorance of
divine truth, which, though it may not stand in the
way of mere animal fervor, is fatal to genuine devotion,
inasmuch as it is the withholding from it its proper aliment. There is the indulgence of wandering thoughts,
which renders what seems to be an act of homage an
act of mockery. There is the neglect of preparatory

meditation, which makes the external duty of prayer too much like the rushing of the horse into battle. Many a Christian, from having neglected to watch against these and other kindred evils, has lost, in a great measure, the spirit of devotion, or else has never possessed it but in so feeble a degree as to render its very existence a matter of question.

In the exact opposite of these evils you may find the most important helps to devotion. Be careful then that you cultivate a habit of spiritual activity, and that your religious affections are kept continually vigorous by proper exercise. Be careful that your mind is richly imbued with divine truth, for it is this which supplies the Christian with arguments in prayer, and which the Holy Spirit uses in teaching him how to pray. Be careful that you keep your heart with all diligence ; for a heart thus kept, awakes as it were instinctively, to the exercise of devotion. Be careful that you bring before your mind, by meditation, the various subjects proper to occupy you in prayer ; for this will render your offering at once more intelligent, more comfortable to yourself, and, as you have reason to believe, more acceptable to God. Indeed there is no Christian duty which you can perform—no Christian grace which you can cultivate, but it is fitted, either directly or indirectly, to cherish a spirit of devotion ; for the various parts of the Christian character are designed to have, and where their tendency is not counteracted, actually do have a reciprocal influence on each other.

Whether you have the spirit of genuine devotion or not, you may ascertain by the following marks. It will lead you to adore the perfections and government of God; to rejoice in the various discoveries of his will; and especially those which are made to us through the medium of his word. It will raise your heart to him in grateful acknowledgment of your entire dependence; in humble confession of the sins of your life, and in devout thanksgiving for the glorious scheme of redemption through Christ. It will lead you to intercede for the whole human family; to pray for the universal prevalence of truth and righteousness; and to aim at a constant conformity to the maxims and principles of the gospel.

The influence which a spirit of devotion, habitually cherished, will exert upon your character, happiness, and usefulness, it is not easy adequately to estimate. The effect of it will indeed be to humble you; for the more the Christian sees of God, the more he is disposed, like Job, to abhor himself, and repent in dust and ashes. But nevertheless it will serve to exalt you; for it will open a free intercourse between you and your Redeemer, and will keep you constantly conversant with the most glorious objects and interests in the universe. It will tend also to render you more pure; for what so likely to effect this as communion with a God of infinite purity? It will serve to enlarge your views, and quicken your faculties, and animate you to the more faithful discharge of every part of your duty. It will be a sure guide to you amidst difficulties, it will bring consolation to you amidst sorrows, and it will render your dying-bed soft as downy pillows are.   In short, it is emphatically the spirit of heaven; and if it have found a lodgement in your heart, it will accompany you thither, and find its appropriate element amidst the harps and songs and hallelujahs of the redeemed.

Your ever devoted

FATHER.

LETTER XX.

CHRISTIAN BENEVOLENCE.

My dear Child—It is the tendency of the gospel not only to elevate the soul to God by bringing into exercise a spirit of devotion, but to minister directly to the benefit of man, by exciting and cherishing a spirit of benevolence. The disposition, naturally amiable and generous, it renders still more so, while it imparts to its exercises a religious character, by subjecting them to the control of principle and conscience. The naturally malevolent spirit it subdues, and changes into a spirit of benignity and good will. It thaws out the heart frozen up by avarice, and unclenches the hand which has been shut against the urgent claims of human woe. It rebukes an indolent temper, and induces a habit of activity by writing on the heart the doctrine of human obligation. In short, wherever the genuine influence of the gospel is felt, there is a spirit of benevolence produced which prompts irresistibly to a course of generous and useful exertion.

That the effect of the gospel upon the human charac-

ter is as I have described, will not be questioned by
any person of common observation or candor. But
while it is readily conceded that it forms in the heart
a spirit of benevolence, the female sex, up to a very
recent period, have, by a sort of common consent, been
in a great measure kept out of the field in which this
spirit may find its legitimate operation. It is true
indeed, that not many years have elapsed since the
church has begun to be aroused to a sense of her obligation. Within considerably less than half a century,
nearly the whole of Protestant Christendom seemed to
be acting upon the conviction that the evangelizing of
the world, instead of being effected by the enlightened
and persevering activity of the church, was to be reserved as a splendid subject for some stupendous miracle. But for some time after the sense of responsibility
began to be felt, and the church began to arise and
shake herself from the slumber of centuries, it was still
a problem in many minds whether this were a proper
field for the pious activity of females; and there were
not a few who pertinaciously maintained that woman
was out of her proper element the moment she emerged
from her retirement into a scene of public benevolent
action. It was indeed her privilege to cultivate benevolent feelings at home, and to dispense charity to
the needy who might come to her door, and go out
occasionally on an exploring tour of mercy in her immediate neighborhood; but as for putting her hand to
the great work of sending the gospel over the world,

it was regarded as something too bold and masculine
to consist with the delicacy of female character.   This
prejudice, I well know, is in a great measure removed,
insomuch that a female who imbibes the actively benevolent spirit of the age, has nothing to fear from
public opinion; nevertheless, I doubt not that, even
at this day there are many who are kept from doing
what they might and what they ought, by an apprehension not unfrequently encouraged by the false delicacy of mothers, that if their activity is carried beyond
a very narrow sphere they will expose themselves to
the charge of being obtrusive.   And while there are
some who urge this plea with sincerity, yet from mistaken views, no doubt there are others who avail themselves of it merely with a view to make themselves
easy and respectable in a habit of indolent inaction.

I cannot suppose it necessary at this day that I
should attempt an argument to convince you that
females are acting within their appropriate sphere
when they are laboring in common with the other sex
for the conversion of the world; for I would fain hope
that instead of requiring to be convinced on this subject, you have already learned to regard it a privilege
and honor to labor in this cause as God may give you
opportunity.   Nevertheless, I admit that the fact of
your belonging to the female sex is not to be overlooked in estimating the part you are to bear in these
great operations.   There are cases in which it may be
proper that both sexes should coöperate in one associa-

tion for the advancement of the same object; and in every instance of this kind propriety requires that females should follow rather than lead: no matter how efficient they are, provided only they keep within proper limits, and are satisfied that the business of directing and managing should be kept in other hands. But, in general, I would recommend that the two sexes should act for these objects in distinct associations, as females particularly will be likely in this way to act with greater freedom and efficiency. Even here, you should of course be on your guard against assuming any thing that does not belong to you; though you should be equally cautious, on the other hand, that you do not, from false modesty, decline any responsibility which you really ought to assume.

That some of the great objects of the present day may enlist the influence and activity of females more appropriately than others, admits not of question; and if there are any which claim their regard before all others, perhaps they are those which more immediately involve the well-being of their own sex. But I know not whether there are scarcely any of the common charities of the day in which females may not with strict propriety bear a part. They may associate for the circulation of the Bible, for the distribution of Tracts, for the education of young men for the Christian ministry, for carrying forward missionary operations, or for any kindred object, and be as little liable to the charge of acting out of their appropriate sphere, as if they were performing the most retired duties of domestic life. In questions of mere political reform, I do not think it the province of females to take a decided part: not that I would prohibit them in all cases from expressing an opinion, but I would object entirely to any thing that even appears like active interference. If they are to exert any influence in this department, it should be of the most silent and unobtrusive kind. But as to those objects which relate merely to the moral and religious improvement of the world, just so far as public sentiment should prevent their taking a part, it would be chargeable with a shameful abridgment of their rights.

In what I have already said, it has been implied that females are to contribute not only their influence, but their substance for the advancement of the Redeemer's cause ; inasmuch as the great work will never go forward without an immense amount of pecuniary aid. How much you shall give is a question to be answered by an enlightened conscience, in view of the means with which God has blessed you. But in forming the estimate of your duty in this respect, take heed that you are not misled by a disposition to indulge the pride of life ; and as the case may be, do not regard some little retrenchment from your personal expenses a hardship, for the sake of casting more liberally into the treasury of the Lord. And while you should make it a matter of conscience to give to the extent of your means, you should also exercise discretion in apportioning your contributions to different objects according to their relative importance. A small contribution made with good judgment as it respects the object, the time, and the manner, may be instrumental of more good than a much larger one made from the mere impulse of a generous spirit, without discrimination and without reflection.

In connection with the great benevolent operations of the age, in which I trust you will never be backward to enlist, let me mention what may at first appear a somewhat humbler sphere of female usefulness. I mean the Sabbath-school. From the time that you cease to be connected with this institution as a pupil, I would have you connected with it as a teacher; and if you discharge your duty faithfully, I may safely say that your labors in this department will be as likely to draw after them a blessing as in any other. The good which female influence has already accomplished by means of this unostentatious institution, it is beyond the power of the human mind adequately to estimate; and it is not too much to say that Sabbath-schools are to hold an important place in the moral machinery by which the world is to be regenerated. However humble may seem the employment of teaching a few children every Sabbath a lesson from the sacred Scriptures, you are probably doing more, at least in many cases, by this simple exercise, to train them for usefulness and for heaven, than is done by all other means united. But in order that you may accomplish all the good of

which this institution is designed to be the medium, take
care that you do your whole duty in connection with
the Sabbath-school with scrupulous fidelity.   Let the
grand object at which you aim be, not only to imbue
the minds of your pupils with scriptural knowledge,
but to imbue their hearts with evangelical feeling ; in
short, to make them practical Bible Christians.   It is
a mistaken principle upon which not only much of the
instruction of the Sabbath-school, but of the family,
has been conducted, that young children are incapable
of being the subjects of converting grace.   A sounder
doctrine on this subject is indeed beginning to prevail ;
and both parents and Sabbath-school teachers are
learning from experience that there is a more impressive meaning than they once supposed in the
Saviour's declaration, "Suffer little children to come
unto me, and forbid them not, for of such is the kingdom of heaven."   Let the instruction that is communicated in the Sabbath-school be entirely evangelical,
and let it be accompanied from time to time, with
tender and solemn appeals to the heart and conscience,
and there is good reason to expect that such a course
of efforts will result in a genuine conversion ; and let
the truth still be impressed from Sabbath to Sabbath,
upon the mind and heart, and let there be direct
counsels and warnings adapted to the circumstances
of the case, and it is reasonable and scriptural to believe, that there will be formed, even in the morning
of life, a stable and consistent Christian character.   It

would seem from some of the prophecies, that, previous
to the opening of the millennium, the influences of the
Spirit are to be plentifully poured out for the conversion of children and youth; and if I do not greatly
mistake the signs of the times, these prophecies are
already beginning to be fulfilled, in the signal success
that attends the Sabbath-school institution.

There is one part of the duty of a Sabbath-school
teacher for which females are especially qualified—
that of finding out and gathering into this nursery of
Christian charity the children of the wretched and
destitute. With more of constitutional tenderness
than belongs to the other sex, they can more readily
gain access to the hearts of parents, and are more
likely to overcome obstacles which may be thrown in
their way. And the visits which they make for the
purpose of bringing in children from the haunts of vice
and misery, may, if properly conducted, in some instances at least, subserve the additional purpose of
communicating good impressions to the parents, and
even of making them regular attendants at the house
of God. There have been repeated instances in which
a young female, not in the highest walks of life, by
faithfully discharging her duty as a Sabbath-school
teacher, both in the school and out of it, has been
honored as the instrument of conversion to a whole
family, and that too a family which had been sunk in
the lowest moral debasement. Surely such facts
ought to encourage every young female who has it in

her power to engage in the Sabbath-school enterprise, and to discharge even those parts of her duty which involve the most self-denial, with alacrity and diligence.

Perhaps there has been no individual in modern times to whom the church is more indebted for elevating the standard of benevolent enterprise in the female sex, than Harriet Newell. When she formed the resolution to encounter the hardships of a missionary life in a heathen land, there were not wanting those, even among professed Christians, to whom the project seemed like the offspring of fanaticism, and who regarded her, when she took leave of her country and kindred, as having well-nigh parted with her reason. But none of these things moved her. With a firmness and disinterestedness of purpose which religion alone could inspire, she turned her back upon all the endearments of home, and after encountering in a long voyage the perils of the deep, reached the anticipated field of her labors. But instead of meeting there the fatigues and deprivations usually incident to missionary life, she found, upon her first arrival, that the hand of death was upon her, and she was sinking suddenly, though calmly, to her rest. But rely on it, she did not cross the ocean and make her grave in that foreign land to no purpose. It looked at first like a dark dispensation, and when it was announced, it seemed as if the whole American church was in tears. But long since has the church been taught to contemplate it as marking one of the brightest eras in the history of her missionary operations. The example of this devoted woman gave a new impulse to female effort in the cause of Christ. Multitudes of her sex have in imagination visited her distant grave, and have felt their hearts kindle with brighter and holier zeal; and while some have followed her in the same enterprise, and have actually laid down their lives on the same field, others have engaged with renewed activity in the cause of their Redeemer at home, and stand ready to make any sacrifice which the honor of his name may require of them. The memory of Harriet Newell is embalmed in thousands of hearts, and no doubt her name will stand on "bright record" through the ages of the millennium; and will shine with the lustre of the firmament when it shall be displayed in the Lamb's book of life.

I know not how to form a greater contrast than must exist between the dying-bed of a female such as I have described, and one who has lived only for purposes of self-gratification. Can you conceive, on the one hand, of any thing more delightful than to look back from a death-bed upon a series of pious efforts for the advancement of the Redeemer's kingdom; to think that those efforts may have been instrumental in opening fountains of salvation in heathen lands; to feel all the composure and joy which the approaching dawn of immortality can shed over the heart; and to look forward to a crown of victory studded with innumerable gems, in each of which you may recognize the ransomed soul of a once perishing heathen? And on the other hand, can you conceive of any thing more dreadful than to review from the gates of the grave a life full of trifling and vanity; to reflect that the world is not the better but the worse for your having lived in it; and to be haunted by the ghosts of departed and misspent years, which come up in frightful succession to give you a deeper chill of horror in the valley of death? If there be any thing alluring or any thing appalling in this contrast, then choose the life of the active Christian, that you may share in his present consolation, and reap his eternal reward.

Your truly affectionate

FATHER.

LETTER XXI.

CHRISTIAN ZEAL.

My dear Child—There is a perpetual tendency in human nature, as well with respect to religion as every thing else, to rush into extremes. And perhaps there is nothing in which this tendency is more strikingly manifested, than in the disposition to magnify one part of Christian character at the expense of another. There are those who make the whole of religion consist in devotional fervor; and by keeping it constantly shut up in the closet, they render it sickly and inefficient. And there are those who make it consist entirely in the stir of public action; who seem to regard the private duties of the Christian as somewhat puritanical; as though they might have been well enough in other days, but in the present age of action have become in some measure outlawed. It hence results, that much of religion that exists in the world is partial; and much of it, for the same reason, spurious.

Now what has happened to every other grace of the Christian has happened to zeal—it has sometimes been elevated to a precedence not only above all the other graces, but at the expense of all the rest; as if it were the sum and substance of Christian character. On the other hand, it has been looked upon with suspicion, and been confounded with enthusiasm, and the first appearance of it has been a signal for alarm, as if the church were falling into a fit of insanity. I shall hope to show you, in the progress of this letter, that while true zeal is absolutely indispensable to a Christian, it still leaves room for the operation of other graces and virtues; and that noble and heavenly as is the genuine quality, there may be much that assumes the name, which, to say the least, will be treated as wood, hay, and stubble.

Christian zeal may be defined in a single sentence as a sincere and warm concern for the glory of God and the spiritual interest of mankind. Let me call your attention more particularly to some of its leading attributes.

It can be scarcely necessary that I should remark that it is a spiritual affection. There is a warm glow of animal feeling which results entirely from constitutional temperament, and which there is great danger, in certain circumstances, of mistaking for Christian zeal. If it happens to be directed towards a good object, as it sometimes is, it may actually accomplish great good, and may work its way through obstacles of an appalling nature, and will not improbably shame some of the more feeble operations of evangelical zeal. But if the object at which it aims is bad, why then its effects will be bad too: it will be as furious and desolating as a whirlwind. It may be enlisted, you perceive, in a good cause or in an evil cause; but not being under the control of principle, it can never be trusted.

Christian zeal, though it may be modified in its operations by constitutional temperament, yet is something entirely distinct from this: it belongs to man only in his renewed state. It is not one of the original qualities which man receives from God the Creator, but one of the spiritual gifts which he receives from God the Sanctifier. It is as truly a Christian grace as faith, or humility, or love to God.

It is another of its characteristics that it is concerned about objects of real moment. There is a zeal which exhausts itself upon rites and forms, and lives in the region of airy speculations and doubtful enterprises. Christian zeal, on the other hand, aims directly at the noblest objects and interests in the universe. It surveys a world lying in wickedness, exposed to God's everlasting curse; it sees on every side a multitude of souls enthralled by the prince of darkness, and liable to sink under his withering frown; and it stretches out the hand of compassion to avert, if possible, the threatening woes, to hedge up the path to destruction, and turn the footsteps of the multitude into the path of life. And it is concerned for the glory of God not less than the happiness of man. It remembers that in every instance in which the redemption of the gospel takes effect, there comes a revenue of glory to God in the highest; and it desires to witness constantly brighter exhibitions of that glory—to behold the Saviour travelling in the greatness of his strength, and gathering gems to his mediatorial crown. Yes, it lifts itself in its sublime aspirations to the very throne of God, and longs and labors for the advancement of all the great and holy interests of his kingdom.

Christian zeal is an enlightened principle. He who is under its influence takes an intelligent view of the great objects he desires to see accomplished, and deliberately satisfies himself of their real importance. He takes a similar view of the means to be employed for their accomplishment, and decides that they are such as reason and conscience and God can approve. And he not only consults faithfully the oracles of God, but seeks direct illumination from above, that in every step he may be guided by heavenly wisdom; and in the most fervent operations of his zeal, he is never for an hour beyond the dominion of sober and enlightened judgment. There is a zeal which is not according to knowledge; which is blind in its operations, and disastrous in its results. But I hardly need say that it has no affinity to the genuine Christian grace.

Christian zeal is earnest. It is not a mere casual emotion, so feeble that it may exist while the mind is scarcely conscious of it; but it is a deep, strong, settled principle, which pervades in its operations the whole soul, and awakens the moral sensibilities into lively exercise. The person who is under its influence has not only an intellectual, but a practical conviction that the salvation of sinners and the interests of Christ's kingdom are matters of the deepest moment; and with this conviction he is earnestly desirous that they should be promoted; and sometimes cannot even rest, or scarcely suffer others to rest, so long as these objects are regarded with indifference.

I know that many of the careless world, and even some professing Christians, whose hearts are bound up in the frost of religious apathy, will stigmatize every appearance of Christian zeal as fanaticism. But I ask, For what objects it is reasonable to be in earnest, if not for the salvation of men and the glory of God? When you contemplate the fearful import of that word eternity, and think what it must be to inherit everlasting joys or to inhabit everlasting burnings; and how many there are on every side who are manifestly rushing towards the pit—I ask whether the lack of earnestness in these circumstances would not indicate infatuation? Christian zeal *is* earnest; and this is one of the reasons why it is rational. It views things as they are, and treats them accordingly.

But it is active, as well as earnest. It is not uncommon to meet with a kind of zeal that expends itself in words—that is satisfied with deploring the spiritual lethargy, or talking about the importance of a revival, or wishing well to the benevolent enterprises of the day. It has a tongue, but it seems to have little of heart, and certainly it is halt and maimed. Christian zeal can and does feel, and it can talk too where there is occasion, but it goes yet further and acts—acts with vigor and efficiency. He who has it comes forward as it were instinctively to the work of the Lord; and whether it be his substance, or his efforts, or his prayers, that are demanded, the contribution is made, and made cheerfully. This is the spirit which you see acted out in the lives of many of our missionaries, and even some of your own sex, who voluntarily surrender all the blessings of civilized society, and make their home in a wilderness or a heathen land, and wear life away in the most self-denying efforts for the salvation of their fellow-creatures. Here you see the *activity* of Christian zeal, a spirit which has its only proper element amidst the wants and miseries of this ruined world.

But notwithstanding its activity, Christian zeal is humble and unobtrusive. It does not indeed shrink from publicity where there is just occasion for making itself public; and such occasions no doubt will often occur; but it does nothing merely to attract observation. Even its highest and holiest triumphs are sometimes obtained in circumstances of retirement; and it takes no pains to trumpet them, even if they are never heard of by the world. Let the Christian accomplish as much by his zeal as he may, even though the whole moral region around him should smile under his influence, he remembers that by the grace of God he is what he is, and that by the grace of God he does what he does; and he chooses to give God all the glory, and to sink down before him as an unworthy instrument. Whenever you see an individual glorying in what he has himself accomplished, and apparently forgetting that in all his efforts he is entirely dependent on the influence of the Spirit, whatever of apparent zeal there may be, you have great reason to question its origin : you have reason to suspect that instead of being a flame kindled from above, it is of the earth, earthy ; or that it originated in a spark from the world below.

Christian zeal is discreet, and has respect to circumstances. I do not mean that it admits of a temporizing policy which will sacrifice principle ; nor a timid policy which makes one walk so softly that not only his footsteps are never heard, but his influence is never felt; but I mean that it is watchful in respect to circumstances and seasons, while it endeavors, so far as possible, to make every thing subservient to the great end of doing good. It does not make a Christian regardless of the common proprieties of life ; it does not decide that the same measures shall be adopted at all times without regard to circumstances; it does not sanction the maxim that the end justifies the means, or that it is no matter whether we obey the directions in God's word or not, provided only the object we have in view is attained ; no, the dictates of Christian zeal are far enough from all this : while it inspires firmness and fearlessness and unyielding resolution, it dictates a spirit of caution, lest by some ill-directed effort the cause should be injured. The grand object it has in view is to accomplish the utmost good by the very means which God has prescribed; and rather than lose sight of that object, it will consent to be nicknamed apathy, or worldly prudence, or any other opprobrious epithet which may be applied to it.

Christian zeal is affectionate. The person who is animated by it will not indeed shrink from the most self-denying duties. One of the most self-denying, in many cases, is that of expostulating with ungodly friends in respect to their salvation; but true zeal will carry a person forward to the discharge of this, even in the most embarrassing circumstances. But while it will cause him to deal honestly and faithfully, it will breathe into his counsels and warnings the genuine spirit of Christian tenderness; and he will show by his whole manner that in all that he does he is influenced by feelings of benevolence and compassion, by an earnest desire to deliver the individual from the greatest possible evils, and to confer upon him the greatest possible blessings. And let me say that the tenderness of Christian zeal does more to render it efficient than almost any other attribute. It is this especially which opens a way into the heart for the entrance of divine truth—which often gains a complete triumph, where the mere energy of zeal would accomplish nothing.

Christian zeal is consistent. It is a truly painful

exhibition, where we see professing Christians acting earnestly, and apparently feeling deeply in reference to some one object, and manifesting an entire apathy in regard to others of equal importance. There are those, for instance, who manifest great zeal in promoting the benevolent operations of the day, who yet take no interest in seeing religion revived in their immediate neighborhood. There are those, again, who seem to be ever awake to the importance of a revival, who are shamefully negligent in respect to their own families, and communicate far less religious instruction to their children than some parents who make no pretensions to piety. And there are those, though the fact may seem almost incredible, who always make conscience of being present at every social meeting, and are ever ready to take part in its exercises, who yet have very little to do with their own closets, and attend with great irregularity upon family devotion. Now all this partial zeal, to say the least, looks suspicious. True Christian zeal differs from this, inasmuch as it directs itself to the whole circle of Christian duties. He who is under its influence, is indeed zealous for the promotion of the benevolent enterprises of the day; but this does not prevent him from taking a deep interest in a revival of religion. He is zealous in coöperating with the Holy Spirit for the salvation of sinners around him; but this does not at all interfere with his desires and efforts to advance the spiritual interests of his own family. He is zealous for supporting religious meetings, not only by his presence, but so far as he is able, by his direct aid; but he is not the less careful to discharge the duties of the closet regularly and devoutly, remembering that if the closet is neglected all the noise and stir he may make about revivals, or in connection with revivals, is mere religious dissipation. He is zealous in all the relations of life. As a parent, he is zealous for the salvation of his children. As a neighbor, he is zealous for those around him. As a member of the church, he is zealous for its prosperity. As a creature of God, redeemed by the blood of his Son, he is zealous for the promotion of his glory. This is the *consistency* of Christian zeal, another attribute which imparts to it much of its loveliness and of its power.

And to crown all, Christian zeal is persevering. It is too much the fashion of the age to wake up and be very active, and perhaps even boisterous for a little season, and then to relapse quietly into the slumber of death; as if during this season of excitement some work of supererogation had been performed, by means of which had been purchased the privilege of a dispensation from all religious feeling and action, at least for a considerable period. And then begins the round of worldliness and of gayety, and of communion with those scenes which are fitted to make the cause of religion bleed; and here is presented to the world—to a world which would gladly find a stumbling-block in every professor—the sad spectacle of a professed disciple of Christ, who was lately seen apparently burning with zeal for the salvation of souls, as dead as a tenant of the grave. I stop not to inquire what must be the effect of such an example—I only say that this is not the zeal which the Bible requires; and though I dare not say that true Christian zeal, owing to the imperfection of human nature, may not be in some degree fluctuating, yet just in proportion as it has this character it becomes justly liable to suspicion. The zeal which is according to knowledge, and which is one of the graces of the Holy Spirit, is a flame which holds on and holds out, and burns brighter and brighter unto the perfect day.

Though I have dwelt at so much length on the nature of Christian zeal, I am unwilling to dismiss the subject without suggesting a few things to enforce its importance.

Let me say then, that it is important as it stands connected with the evidence of personal piety. It is not easy, I acknowledge, to say to what extent an individual may be deficient in this grace, and yet be a true Christian; but that some degree of it is essential to Christian character, admits of no question; and if you possess it in only a feeble measure, so that its existence shall be a matter of doubt, your evidences, to say the least, must be far from being satisfactory. You may be saved at the last, but you cannot consistently indulge more than a faint and trembling hope of salvation. Do you desire to have bright evidence that you are to dwell with God for ever? Then rise up to a high tone of Christian zeal.

But this grace has much to do with religious enjoyment. This indeed may be inferred from the remark already made; for the Christian's enjoyment is so intimately connected with his evidences, that whatever obscures the latter, must, in the same degree, diminish the former. But the point to which I here especially refer is, that Christian zeal is necessary to the free and comfortable discharge of duty. Without it I know it is possible to go through a round of external duties, to be in the church and the prayer-meeting, and even in the closet at stated seasons, and occasionally to drop a word of warning upon the ear of a sinner, and put forth a hand to move forward the great moral machinery of the age; but it will be more like a reluctant service rendered to a taskmaster, than the cheerful homage of filial affection. On the other hand, let the heart glow with Christian zeal, and the hands will of course be nerved for Christian effort; even the most difficult duties will become easy, and the most appalling obstacles will vanish. Whoever then would perform the duties and endure the trials of the religious life with ease and comfort, must become richly imbued with Christian zeal.

And this grace is not less essential to the Christian's usefulness than to his enjoyment. For without zeal or with little of it, supposing him to be a Christian, how limited will be the good which he will accomplish!

Admitting that he is to be saved himself, yet perhaps not a single soul will be saved by his instrumentality. Who is the individual that exerts an influence in raising the tone of public morals by purifying and elevating public sentiment? It is he whose heart is fired with Christian zeal. Who is the person to be instrumental in producing or sustaining a revival of religion; or in sending the gospel abroad to the destitute; or in carrying forward any of the high and holy operations connected with the kingdom of Christ? It is the Christian who is full of holy zeal. And who are they who in coming years are to be honored with the chief instrumentality in the conversion of the world? Who are they that will be greeted as having done most for Christ when the glories of the millennial morning shall be spread over the earth? I tell you, they are your truly zealous Christians—men and women who were not afraid of being bold lest they should be accounted rash, or prudent lest they should be accounted timid, or earnest lest they should be called fanatics. If you desire to have a part in bringing God's glorious purposes to their accomplishment—if you desire to escape the doom of the slothful servant, and to appear at last to have lived for the benefit of your fellow-creatures and the glory of God, be fervently zealous in the Redeemer's cause.

I will only add that this grace is important as it stands connected with the Christian's final reward. True it is that reward is of grace, and not of debt.

Even the brightest crown that shall sparkle through all the ranks of the redeemed, will be altogether the purchase of the Redeemer's blood, and in no sense the earnings of human merit. Nevertheless, the crowns of heaven will be distributed according to what each has been and done in the service of Christ. That Christian who has been actuated during a whole life by a glowing zeal for the salvation of men and the honor of the Redeemer, will shine as the brightness of the firmament, while the more sluggish Christian will be saved so as by fire. Do you desire then not only to inhabit the world of glory, but to rise to a high place in that world? Would you stand near the throne of God and shout the praises of redemption in the loudest, sweetest, holiest strains that vibrate around the arch of heaven? Would you aspire to an intimate companionship with angels, and to all the purity and bliss of which your nature is susceptible? I say again, let your heart and your life furnish a perpetual exhibition of living, glowing, efficient zeal.

I am, as ever, your devoted

FATHER.

LETTER XXII.

IMPROVEMENT OF TIME.

My dear Child—The subject upon which I am now to address you, may be considered as including, in a general sense, much to which I have already directed your attention; for you will instantly perceive that, as your time is given you to be filled up with the discharge of duty, so the right improvement of it must involve a faithful attention to all the duties connected with your various relations. The general subject however is of so much importance that I do not feel willing to pass it over without bringing it distinctly before you.

There is a fashion which prevails too extensively among all classes, of killing time; and as this is an evil into which many persons, and even many professing Christians fall without being aware of it, it may not be amiss that I should put you on your guard, by mentioning some of the ways in which life is frittered away without the accomplishment of its object.

One very effectual means of killing time is by sleep.

It is true, indeed, that a certain degree of sleep is necessary alike to the physical and intellectual constitution : it is the kind restorer of the human faculties from a state of exhaustion, and is an evidence alike of the wisdom and goodness of God. No doubt also an individual may err in taking too little repose ; as he may thus not only abridge his period of usefulness, but his amount of exertion during that period : for if he bring to his work, no matter what it is, faculties that have lost their elasticity through the want of sleep, he may indeed keep himself busy, but there is reason to fear that he will be busied in a way that will be little better than killing time. But the error to which I designed here to refer, is that of excessive indulgence in sleep. And the evil of this in respect to the loss of time is twofold : not only the time which is occupied by sleep is lost, but the mind acquires a habit of drowsiness or indolence, which greatly abates the vigor of all its operations. That different constitutions may require different degrees of rest, there can be no doubt ; how much is necessary in any given case is to be ascertained only by experiment ; and every one ought to make it a matter of conscience to consume as little time in this way as is consistent with the most healthful and vigorous state of the faculties.

Another means not less effectual of killing time, is the indulgence of a wandering imagination. It is an employment to which some minds are exceedingly attached, to suffer their thoughts to wander uncontrolled in any direction they may happen to take. Sometimes they may fall into one channel and sometimes into another; but let them assume whatever course they may, no effort is made to direct or restrain them.   To say nothing of the fact that where such a habit exists there must be many trains of thought which could not be uttered without an offence to the purity and even the decorum of virtue, there can be no doubt that nearly all these operations of the mind partake deeply of vanity, and are unworthy of an accountable and immortal being.   At the same time, useless and sinful as this employment is in itself, it occupies the fleeting moments of man's probation—moments that were given him to prepare for eternity.

I may instance vain conversation as another means of frittering away time.   The social principle which was implanted for the most important purposes, is too often brought into operation for purposes which God and reason and conscience unitedly condemn.   But to say nothing of the more flagrant vices of the tongue, who does not know how strong is the tendency, I may say, in most persons, to indulge in idle and frivolous discourse?   Such a habit is exceedingly fitted to dissipate the mind; but the least you can say of it is, that it is attended by a criminal waste of time.   It is robbing one's own understanding and heart: it is robbing God.

And the same evil is accomplished by light and foolish reading.   I have elsewhere dwelt so much upon this, that I allude to it here only as it stands connected with the loss of time.   And there are no persons probably who are more liable to fall into this error than young females.   Many of them will even consent to deprive themselves of sleep for the sake of going through with some ridiculous love-story, or following out the fortunes of some imaginary hero, as they are depicted in a novel.   If you should ever find yourself engaged in this miserable employment, just pause, at least long enough to inquire of your conscience whether that be the purpose for which your precious time was given you.

But if you would do your whole duty on this subject, you must not only avoid the evil of which I have been speaking, but you must actually use your time to the best advantage.   Here again, suffer me to give you two or three directions.

Be careful that your time is employed upon objects of real utility.   It is possible that an individual may be very active, and in a certain way may bring much to pass, and yet, after all, may have no good account to render of his time, inasmuch as it has been bestowed upon objects of little or no moment.   It is not enough that the object to which your efforts are directed should not directly interfere with the interests of any of your fellow-creatures, or that it should exert no positively bad influence upon yourself: it should be something from which you or they may reap some positive advantage.   In selecting a sphere in which to occupy your time, you ought indeed to have respect to your peculiar talents; but you should be certain that it is a sphere of real usefulness.

If you would use your time to the best advantage, I hardly need say that you must form a habit of persevering diligence. This is essential, not only because you thus crowd into a given period the greatest amount of useful exertion, but because the faculties are thereby improved, and rendered capable of more vigorous and successful exercise. Make it a rule, therefore, never to allow yourself to be idle, when your health and circumstances will permit you to be active. If you once form an industrious habit, you will never afterwards be able to content yourself in a state of inactivity; and on the other hand, if you begin life with a habit of indolence, you will probably never after acquire a relish for vigorous exertion. In whatever circumstances Providence may place you, take care that the whole of your time be employed; and consider the first inroads of indolence as a melancholy harbinger of the wreck of your usefulness and the loss of your reputation.

There is one caution however which I would suggest in connection with this point—it is, that you should never suffer yourself to be in a hurry. Let the demands upon your time be ever so numerous, endeavor to keep your mind perfectly composed, and address yourself to your various avocations as calmly as if you were insensible of their pressure. The moment you become agitated by care, you well-nigh lose the power of doing any thing to purpose. Your thoughts under such an influence, will fly off to the winds, and a distracted state of feeling will ensue, which will effectually palsy every effort. Be as diligent as your health will admit, but never suffer your exertions to be embar-rassed by the apprehension that you have more on your hands than you shall be able to accomplish.

And this leads me to say that very much will depend on your having your duties, so far as possible, reduced to system. There is a way which many good people have of taking things at random ; seeming to be satis-fied if they are only in a field of usefulness, whether they are laboring to the best advantage or not. In-stead of taking a deliberate survey of the field into which they are cast, and the various duties which de-volve upon them, and assigning to each set of duties an appropriate time, they take every thing as it hap-pens to rise ; and as a matter of course, not unfre-quently find themselves overwhelmed by such an accu-mulation of cares, that they are in precisely the state of which I have just spoken—they know not to which duty to give the precedence. If you take care to cultivate order in the discharge of your duties, you will not only accomplish more, and accomplish it with greater ease, but there will grow out of it a beautiful consistency of character, which will of itself be an important means of usefulness.

If you need motives to urge you to the faithful

improvement of your time, let me remind you of your responsibility to God. Your time is one of the talents which he has intrusted to you, and for which he will ere long call you to an account. Each moment is part of the precious deposit; and it bears its report for or against you to the bar of your final Judge. Remember that he requires that your whole time should be spent in his service 'and to his glory. If you would meet him to render an account of your stewardship with confidence and joy, see to it that you practically recognize his claim, and live under an abiding sense of your obligation.

Recollect too, that the improvement of your time is immediately connected with the improvement of all your other talents. If your time is wasted, so also is the vigor of your intellect; your powers of speech are perverted; your moral and religious privileges abused; and your whole influence turned into an improper channel. If you waste your whole time, you of course throw yourself into a current that will bear you rapidly to perdition: just in proportion as you waste your time, you accumulate materials for a fearful reckoning, and if you are a professed Christian, you render it probable that your hope will be as the giving up of the ghost.

Remember further, that the time is short. Should your life be protracted to the period of old age, you will say, at its close, that it was only "as a watch of the night, as a dream when one awaketh." But of this you can have no assurance; and the only conclusion which analogy warrants is, that you will probably not reach an advanced period. And need I say that even now some of your last moments may be on the wing? Has the improvement of your past life been such that you can review it with peace and approbation?

But after death is the judgment. When time is past, then comes eternity; and your improvement of the one must lay a foundation for your condition in the other. With this solemn thought, I take leave of the subject, earnestly praying that your time may be spent in such a manner that it shall be good for you and for others that you have lived.

Your affectionate

FATHER.

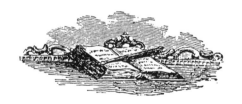

LETTER XXIII.

PREPARATION FOR DEATH.

MY DEAR CHILD—There is scarcely any thing in human experience which at first view strikes the mind as so difficult to be accounted for, as the utter insensibility which the mass of mankind manifest on the subject of death.   That death is an event of most solemn and momentous import, whether it be regarded in its physical or its moral bearings, no rational mind can question.   Nature herself renders a testimony to this truth in that shrinking and shuddering which the spirit feels when it is actually entering into communion with this king of terrors.   But who, with an eye upon the world, can fail to perceive that this event is but little thought of; and though the grave itself is continually speaking forth its rebuke to human thoughtlessness and infatuation, and though friendship, strong and tender in death, often pours out its earnest expostulations to the living to prepare to die, yet the mass of the world slumber on till they are startled by the footsteps of that messenger whose mandate they cannot

resist. This surely is not wisdom. It shows the desperate madness of the human heart. It shows that
man is guilty, that he is afraid to hold communion
with the future, to enter into the secret chambers of
his own soul, and ponder the prospect of a retribution.

But if the great majority of mankind manifest an
absolute aversion to the contemplation of death, it
must be acknowledged that even those who profess to
be the disciples of Christ, and to regard death as gain,
do not live as might be expected in view of it. They
think of it too little, converse about it too little, prepare for it too little. Here again, the secret of this
is, that they love this world too well, and even though
they are partially sanctified, they have too little sympathy with the objects and interests and glories of the
world which the eye of faith sees beyond it.

There is a preparation for death which devolves
upon the unforgiven sinner, of mighty import. There
is charged against him in the book of God's remembrance an awful catalogue of crimes, which he can do
nothing in the way of merit to expiate. His heart is
the seat of corrupt propensities and affections, which
render him utterly incapable of the joys of holiness.
If he die with this character, nothing awaits him but
that indignation and wrath which the Bible has de-
nounced upon the ungodly. His preparation for death,
therefore, must consist in having his offences cancelled
by the blood of Christ, and his heart renewed by the
Spirit of Christ ; in other words, in a compliance with

the requisitions of the gospel, by repentance towards God and faith in the Lord Jesus Christ. These requisitions once obeyed, he is in the most important sense prepared to die. It is not indeed certain that he will die triumphantly, or even die peacefully, for he is yet but a babe in Christ; but it is as certain as the testimony of the Highest can make it, that he will die to live and reign with the Redeemer on his throne for ever.

There is also a preparation for death, though of a somewhat modified character, that devolves upon the Christian. For notwithstanding the soul which has once experienced the transforming power of the Holy Spirit is sealed to the day of redemption, yet it has still much of remaining corruption to struggle with, and is far from being adorned with the beauty of perfect holiness. With the Christian, then, preparation for death consists not merely in possessing a principle of grace, but in keeping it in lively exercise; not merely in being able to recur to seasons in which the love of Christ was shed abroad in his heart, but to feel the precious influence of this love daily and habitually. It is true, as I have said, that every believer dies a safe death; but it is not true that every one dies in the exercise of a triumphant and elevated faith; and some, no doubt, as a chastisement for their neglect of duty, are left to die under a cloud; and perhaps are in actual horror, till they emerge from the cloud which their own guilt has spread over them, into the bright light of an everlasting day. Every believer ought, every believer may avoid the evil of dying in darkness. Let him keep his lamp trimmed and burning, and his passage through the valley of death will brighten into a scene of heavenly illumination.

You cannot fail to perceive that it is a matter of infinite moment that you are prepared to die—prepared in such a sense that the thought of death shall never be unwelcome, and the approach of it, however unexpected, instead of filling you with alarm, shall be hailed as the harbinger of heavenly glory. I am sure that you aim at something higher than even to die safely: you desire that your death may speak forth the all-sustaining power of the gospel; that in dying you may bring some honor to Him whose death is the price of all your hopes and joys, of your entire redemption. Let me then give you two or three brief directions to aid you in making this most desirable attainment.

Meditate frequently and solemnly upon death. If it comes up before the mind only occasionally, and at distant intervals, the certain consequence will be that it will be regarded with chilling apprehension; and your thoughts will be likely to fly from it, even though reason and conscience strive to detain them. Let no day, especially let no evening pass, which does not witness to your visiting in thought the grave. Endeavor to become familiar with this subject in its various parts and bearings. Meditate on the certainty of the change ; on the nearness of its approach ; on the circumstances which will probably attend it ; the parting with friends, the dropping of the earthly tabernacle, the pains, the groans, the dying strife, which may be crowded into the last hour ; on the amazing scenes which must open upon the spirit the moment death has done its work, and on the riches of that grace which secures to the believer a complete victory in his conflict, and a triumphant entrance into heaven.   Let this course of meditation be conducted in the most practical manner possible ; let it all come home to your own bosom as a matter of personal concern ; and the effect of it will be to make the world appear in its true light, and to transfer from time to time some new affections from earth to heaven.

Beware of the world.   Beware of its seductive flatteries, its pestilential maxims, its unhallowed practices. Remember that the spirit of the world is directly opposed to the spirit of the gospel ; and that both cannot find a permanent lodgement in the same bosom.   If the world attempt to seduce you by its smiles, dally not with the tempter for a moment.   If it attempt by its frowns to wither your good purposes and bring you into subjection, in the strength of almighty grace march forward to the conflict, and the world will retire and leave you the victory.   Have as little to do with the grovelling and polluted scenes of earth as you can, in consistency with your duty.   Rise above the world and try to breathe the atmosphere of heaven.

Thus you will use it as not abusing it; and all you have to do with it, instead of retarding, will actually advance your preparation for the grave.

And instead of multiplying directions on this subject, I may say all in one word, if you would be prepared to die, cultivate a spirit of devoted piety. Aim constantly at the fulness of the stature of a perfect person in Christ. Let every Christian grace be in you and abound; endeavor to let it be in you in its utmost perfection. Give to the Saviour the unreserved homage of your heart, and the entire obedience of your life. Follow him through good report and bad report, and count it a joy and an honor to bear his cross. Let your soul always be a temple for the Holy Ghost, and be filled with the fulness of God. Such a life constitutes true preparation for death. Live thus, and you will have nothing to do in your last hour but to-resign your spirit into your Redeemer's hands and die rejoicing.

With these brief directions, designed to aid you in your preparation for death, I now take my leave of you. And surely there is no subject with which I might more properly conclude these letters; for this is the point in which they are all designed to terminate. Whatever other purpose might be answered by them, it would be with me a matter of little moment, provided they should have no effect in preparing you for death and eternity. I here repeat what I said at the beginning, that though you should possess every amiable quality, and every accomplishment which your friends could desire, I could contemplate your condition only with the deepest concern and sorrow, if I were compelled to regard you a stranger to godliness, and exposed to perdition.

Let me entreat you then, my dear child, as you regard the tenderest sensibilities of a father's heart, as you regard the hopes which were formed in respect to you by a mother who loved you and blessed you in death, and as you regard the wishes and prayers of another mother, who has watched over your infancy, and cherished and counselled your childhood—let me entreat you to endeavor to conform your character to the standard which has been exhibited in these letters. Let me only see this, and I am sure I shall never cease to bless God that I have written them. Give me but this joy, and though I should be called to leave you while you are yet young, in this cold, ungrateful world, I could leave you without a chill of apprehension, fully persuaded that you would enjoy the gracious protection of God while here, and mingle in the refined and noble communion of the redeemed hereafter.

That the perpetual blessing of a covenant-keeping God may rest upon you, is the most earnest prayer of
Your devoted
FATHER.